The End of Forgetting

The End of Forgetting

Growing Up with Social Media

KATE EICHHORN

 Harvard University Press

Cambridge, Massachusetts

London, England

2019

First printing

Library of Congress Cataloging-in-Publication Data

Names: Eichhorn, Kate, 1971– author.

Title: The end of forgetting : growing up with social media / Kate Eichhorn.

Description: Cambridge, Massachusetts : Harvard University Press, 2019. |
    Includes bibliographical references and index.

Identifiers: LCCN 2018050010 | ISBN 9780674976696 (alk. paper)

Subjects: LCSH: Social media—Psychological aspects. | Online identities. |
    Internet and children. | Internet and youth.

Classification: LCC HM742 .E43 2019 | DDC 302.23/1—dc23

LC record available at https://lccn.loc.gov/2018050010

CONTENTS

Introduction

Growing Up at the End of Forgetting

n the twentieth century, if one was truly mortified by a photograph from childhood or adolescence, there was a simple solution: secretly slip the photograph out of its frame or the family photo album and destroy it. In seconds, a particularly awkward event or stage of one's life could be effectively erased. The photograph's absence might eventually have been noticed, but in the analogue era, unless one's relatives were fastidious enough to preserve the negative, one could be more or less assured that once the photograph was ripped up or burned, this embarrassing trace of the past had vanished. Without the photograph's presence, one could also assume that any lingering memories of the event or stage of life would soon fade in one's own mind and, perhaps more importantly, in the minds of others. In retrospect, this vulnerability to human emotion—to the shame and anger that once led us to destroy photographs with our bare hands—may have been one of the great yet underappreciated features of analogue media.

Several decades into the age of digital media, the ability to leave one's childhood and adolescent years behind, along with the likelihood of having others forget one's younger self, are now imperiled. While young people may still covertly attempt to delete photographs of themselves from their parents' and grandparents' mobile phones, tablets, and computers, that act is in no way akin to ripping a photograph out of an album and tossing it into the fireplace. It is nearly impossible to know whether the image is gone for good. Does the embarrassing photograph exist on only a single device? Has it already been shared with dozens of friends and relatives? Did anyone find it cute or amusing enough to post on Facebook? Where has the photograph circulated? Could all the copies be retrieved and destroyed? Worse yet, was the photograph tagged? An act of destruction that once took mere seconds is now a massive and nearly impossible undertaking.

Of course, it is unfair to blame this current phenomenon on the digital hoarding of doting parents and grandparents. After all, children and teens are now generating their own photographs at an unprecedented rate. Although exact numbers are hard to come by, it is evident that a majority of young people with access to mobile phones take and circulate selfies on a daily basis.[1] There is also growing evidence that selfies are not simply a tween and teen obsession. Toddlers enjoy taking selfies, too, and whether intentionally or unintentionally, have even managed to put their images into circulation.[2] But what is the cost of this excessive documentation? More specifically, what does it mean to come of age in an era when images of childhood and adolescence, and even the social networks formed during this fleeting period of life, are so easily preserved and may stubbornly persist with or without one's intention or desire? Can one ever transcend one's youth if it remains perpetually present? These are the urgent questions that this book seeks to explore.

From the "Disappearance of Childhood" to Perpetual Childhood

The crisis we face concerning the persistence of childhood images was the least of concerns when digital technologies began to restructure our everyday lives in the early 1990s. Media scholars, sociologists, educational researchers, and alarmists of all political stripes were more likely to bemoan the loss of childhood than to worry about the prospect of childhood's perpetual presence. In 1994, as the general public was just beginning to understand and absorb an entirely new vocabulary that included concepts such as "the Internet," "cyberspace," and "the World Wide Web," I was beginning my graduate studies in the field of education. Educational researchers at that time were obsessed with measuring, monitoring, and debating the impact of the internet on youth and, more broadly, on the future of education. My supervisor, whose previous work had focused on the history of literacy, encouraged me to throw away my books, learn to code, and start researching and developing educational video games for the future "wired classroom." Her optimism was unusual. A few educators and educational researchers were earnestly exploring the potential benefits of the internet and other emerging digital technologies, but the period was marked by widespread moral panic about new media technologies. As a result, much of the earliest research on young people and the internet sought either to support or to refute fears about what was about to unfold online.

Some of the early concerns about the internet's impact on children and adolescents were legitimate. The internet did make pornography, including violent pornography, more available, and it enabled child predators to more easily gain access to young people. Law enforcement agencies and legislators continue to grapple with these serious problems. However, many early concerns about the internet were rooted in fear alone and were informed by longstanding assumptions about youth and their ability to make rational decisions.

Many adults feared that if left to surf the web alone, children would suffer a quick and irreparable loss of innocence. These concerns were fueled by reports about what allegedly lurked online.[3] At a time when many adults were just beginning to venture online, the internet was still commonly depicted in the popular media as a place where anyone could easily wander into a sexually charged multiuser domain (MUD), hang out with computer hackers and learn the tricks of their criminal trade, or hone their skills as a terrorist or bomb builder. In fact, doing any of these things usually required more than a single foray onto the web. But that did little to curtail perceptions of the internet as a dark and dangerous place where threats of all kinds were waiting at the welcome gate.

While the media obsessed over how to protect children from online pornography, perverts, hackers, and vigilantes, researchers in the applied and social sciences were busy producing reams of evidence-based studies on the supposed link between internet use and various physical and social disorders. Some researchers cautioned that spending too much time online would lead to greater levels of obesity, repetitive strain, tendonitis, and back injuries in young people. Others cautioned that the internet caused mental problems, ranging from social isolation and depression to a decreased ability to distinguish between real life and simulated situations.[4]

A common theme underpinning both popular and scholarly articles about the internet in the 1990s was that this new technology had created a shift in power and access to knowledge. A widely reprinted 1993 article ominously titled "Caution: Children at Play on the Information Highway" warned, "Dropping children in front of the computer is a little like letting them cruise the mall for the afternoon. But when parents drop their sons or daughters off at a real mall, they generally set ground rules: Don't talk to strangers, don't go into Victoria's Secret, and here's the amount of money you'll be able to spend. At the electronic mall, few parents are setting the rules or even have a clue about how to set them."[5] If parents were simultaneously concerned and clueless, it had much to do with the fact that as the decade wore on, young people grew to outnumber adults in many regions of what was then still commonly described as cyberspace. Practical parental questions became increasingly challenging to answer and, in some cases, even to ask: Who had the power to impose a curfew in this online realm? Where were the boundaries of this new and rapidly expanding space? And what sorts of relationships were children establishing there? Were young people who met online simply pen pals who exchanged letters in real time, or were they actual acquaintances? Could one's child have sexual encounters, or just exchange messages about sex online? There was nothing new about parents worrying about where their children were and what they were doing, but these worries were exacerbated by new conceptual challenges. Parents were now having to make informed decisions about their children's well-being in a realm that few of them understood or had even experienced firsthand.

In such a context, it is easy to understand why the imperiled innocence of children was invoked as a rationale for increased regulation and monitoring of the internet. In the United States, the Communications Decency Act, signed into law by President Clinton in 1996, gained considerable support due to widespread fears that without increased regulation of communications, the nation's children were doomed to become perverts and digital vigilantes. The act, which the American Civil Liberties Union would later successfully challenge in the Supreme Court as a violation of the First Amendment, authorized the U.S. government to "encourage the development of technologies which maximize user control over what information is received by individuals, families, and schools who use the Internet and other interactive computer services" and "to remove disincentives for the development and utilization of blocking and filtering technologies that empower parents to restrict their children's access to objectionable or inappropriate online material."[6] Those who drafted the act took at face value the claim that children's perception of reality is invariably influenced by their interactions with media technologies (a claim based on earlier studies of young people's interactions with film and television), and as a result, filters are necessary.

At least a few critics, however, recognized that discourses centered on children's innocence were being used to promote online censorship without taking children's actual needs into account. In a 1997 article published in *Radical Teacher*, the media theorist Henry Jenkins astutely observed that parents', educators', and politicians' moral panic over the internet was nothing new. From attacks on comic books in the early twentieth century to later panics about the negative effects of cinema, radio, and television, the argument that new media pose a threat to young people was already well rehearsed. Jenkins argued that the real problem was not the new media, but rather the myth of childhood innocence itself:

The myth of "childhood innocence" "empties" children of any thoughts of their own, stripping them of their own political agency and social agendas so that they may become vehicles for adult needs, desires, and politics. . . . The "innocent" child is an increasingly dangerous abstraction when it starts to substitute in our thinking for actual children or when it helps justify efforts to restrict real children's minds and to regulate their bodies. The myth of "childhood innocence," which sees children only as potential victims of the adult world or as beneficiaries of paternalistic protection, opposes pedagogies that empower children as active agents in the educational process. We cannot teach children how to engage in critical thought by denying them access to challenging information or provocative images.[7]

Jenkins was not the only one to insist that the real challenge was to empower children and adolescents to use the internet in productive and innovative ways so as to build a new and vibrant public sphere. We now know that a critical mass of educators and parents did choose to allow children ample access to the internet in the 1990s and early 2000s. Those young people ended up building many of the social media and sharing economy platforms that would transform the lives of people of all ages by the end of the first decade of the new millennium. (In 1996, Facebook's Mark Zuckerberg was twelve years old, and Airbnb's Brian Chesky was fifteen.) But at the time, Jenkins had a hard sell—his argument was circulating in a culture where many people had already given up on the future of childhood. Among the more well-known skeptics was another media theorist, Neil Postman.

Postman argued in his 1982 book *The Disappearance of Childhood* that new media were eroding the distinction between childhood and adulthood. "With the electric media's rapid and egalitarian disclosure of the total content of the adult world, several profound consequences result," he claimed. These consequences included a diminishment of the authority of adults and the curiosity of children.[8] Although not necessarily invested in the idea of childhood innocence, Postman was invested in the idea and ideal of childhood, which he believed was already in decline. This, he contended, had much to do with the fact that childhood—a relatively recent historical invention—is a construct that has always been deeply entangled with the history of media technologies.

While there have, of course, always been young people, a number of scholars have posited that the concept of childhood is an early modern invention. Postman not only adopted this position but also argued that this concept was one of the far-reaching consequences of movable type, which first appeared in Mainz, Germany, in the late fifteenth century.[9] With the spread of print culture, orality was demoted, creating a hierarchy between those who could read and those who could not. The very young were increasingly placed outside the adult world of literacy. During this period, something else occurred: different types of printed works began to be produced for different types of readers. In the sixteenth century, there were no age-based grades or corresponding books. New readers, whether they were five or thirty-five, were expected to read the same basic books.[10] By the late eighteenth century, however, the world had changed. Children had access to children's books, and adults had access to adult books. Children were now regarded as a separate category that required protection from the evils of the adult world. But the reign of childhood (according to Postman, a period running roughly from the mid-nineteenth to the mid-twentieth centuries) would prove short-lived. Although earlier communications technologies and broadcasting mediums, from the telegraph to cinema, were already chipping away at childhood, the arrival of television in the mid-twentieth century marked the beginning of the end. Postman concludes, "Television erodes the dividing line between childhood and adulthood in three ways, all having to do with its undifferentiated accessibility: first, because it requires no instruction to grasp its form; second, because it does not make complex demands on either mind or behavior; and third, because it does not segregate its audience."[11]

Although Postman's book focuses on television, it contains a curious but rarely discussed side note on the potential impact of computing. In the final chapter, Postman poses and responds to six questions, including the following: "Are there any communication technologies that have the potential to sustain the need for childhood?" In response to his own question, he replies, "The only technology that has this capacity is the computer." To program a computer, he explains, one must in essence learn a language, a skill that would have to be acquired in childhood: "Should it be deemed necessary that everyone must know how computers work, how they impose their special world-view, how they alter our definition of judgment—that is, should it be deemed necessary that there be universal computer literacy—it is conceivable that the schooling of the young will increase in importance and a youth culture different from adult culture might be sustained." But things could turn out differently. If economic and political interests decide that they would be better served by "allowing the bulk of a semiliterate population to entertain itself with the magic of visual computer games, to use and be used by computers without understanding . . . childhood could, without obstruction, continue on its journey to oblivion."[12]

At the time, Postman's argument no doubt made a lot of sense. When he was writing his book—likely in longhand or on a typewriter—the idea that a future generation of children, even toddlers, would easily be able to use computers had not yet occurred to most people. In 1982, when *The Disappearance of Childhood* hit the shelves, the graphical user interface that would transform computing had yet to be launched on a mass scale. Unless Postman happened to have had access to a rare Xerox Star, which retailed for about $16,000 per unit in 1981, he presumably was not thinking about computers in their current form at all. He likely imagined that using computers for more than play would remain the purview of those with considerable expertise (an expertise akin to mastering a new language). Of course, this is not how the digital revolution played out.

As the Xerox Star evolved into today's familiar computing interface and later into the touch screens of mobile phones and tablets, the ability to program computers was no longer linked to the ability to use computers for a wide range of purposes beyond gaming. Thanks to Xerox's graphical user interface, eventually popularized by Apple, by the 2000s one could do many things with computers without knowledge of or interest in their inner workings. The other thing that Postman did not anticipate is that young people would be more adept at building and programming computers than most older adults. Fluency in this new language, unlike most other languages, did not deepen or expand with age. By the late 1990s, there was little doubt that adults were not in control of the digital revolution. The most ubiquitous digital tools and platforms of our era, from Google to Facebook to Airbnb, would all be invented by people just out of their teens. What was the result? In the end, childhood as it once existed (i.e., in the pre-television era) was not restored, but Postman's fear that childhood would disappear also proved wrong. Instead, something quite unexpected happened.

In the early 1980s, Postman and many others saw the line between children's culture and adults' culture rapidly dissolving, primarily because of the undifferentiating impact of television. The solution was to restore the balance—to reestablish the boundaries between these once separate cultures. Postman argued that if we could return to a pre-television era where children occupied one world and adults another, childhood might have some hope of surviving into the twenty-first century and well beyond. Today, the distinction between childhood and adulthood has reemerged, but not in the way that Postman imagined.

In our current digital age, child and adolescent culture is alive and well. Most young people spend hours online every day exploring worlds in which most adults take little interest and to which they have only limited access. But this is where the real difference lies. In the world of print, adults determined what children could and could not access—after all, adults operated the printing presses, purchased the books, and controlled the libraries. Now, children are free to build their own worlds and, more importantly, to populate these worlds with their own content. The content, perhaps not surprisingly, is predominantly centered on the self (the selfie being emblematic of this tendency). So, in a sense, childhood has survived, but its nature— what it is and how it is experienced and represented—is increasingly in the hands of young people themselves. If childhood was once constructed and recorded by adults and mirrored back to children (e.g., in a carefully curated family photo album or a series of home video clips), this is no longer the case. Today, young people create images and put them into circulation without the interference of adults.

And this brings us back to the problem with which this book seeks to grapple. In sharp contrast to Postman's prediction, childhood never did disappear. Instead, it has become ubiquitous in a new and unexpected way. Today, childhood and adolescence are more visible and pervasive than ever before. As I show throughout this book, this is largely due to the fact that for the first time in history, children and adolescents have widespread access to the technologies needed to represent their lives, circulate these representations, and forge networks with each other, often with little or no adult supervision. The potential danger is no longer childhood's disappearance, but rather the possibility of a perpetual childhood. The real crisis of the digital age is not the disappearance of childhood, but the specter of a childhood that can never be forgotten.

Forgotten Childhoods and Childhoods without End

Not everyone fears a world in which the past is difficult, if not impossible, to shake off. Indeed, many people relish their childhood memories and regret having failed to save more mementos and photographs of their early years. Still others wonder why their parents did not save these precious traces on their behalf. There are also specific experiences of longing for the past that result from periods of conflict, forced displacement, or mass migration. Many people born in Europe in the 1930s to 1940s, for example, grew up with the notable absence of early family photographs, which their families had been forced to abandon as they fled their homes or were forcibly displaced.[13] Now, perhaps for the first time, it is possible to wonder whether such absences will exist at all in the future. Before further considering what it might mean to live in a world where one's childhood and adolescence remain forever present—a world where one's early digital footprints lurk alongside one's adult self—it is useful to briefly examine just how remarkably different things were only a few decades ago, when the parents and grandparents of today's children were coming of age.

Many people growing up in the mid-twentieth century lacked documentation of their childhood. Some families were forced to leave photographs and other mementos behind as a result of political conflicts, but in other cases, there may have been no photographs to pack up at all. Although photography was already widely accessible to the average middle-class family, it was still not unusual to grow up without any, or with only minimal, documentary traces of the past.[14]

The trauma of World War II led not only to gaps in documentation but also to selective gaps in memory. Many people of my generation—those born in the 1960s and 1970s—grew up with parents and grandparents who chose to keep the past largely or entirely hidden. Some Jewish families opted to raise their children without mentioning that they were Holocaust survivors or even that they were Jewish.[15] An even larger percentage of German families opted to raise their children without mentioning what they had been doing or where they were during the war. From the 1950s to the 1980s, it was still possible for families to harbor such secrets. A Jewish family could pretend they had never been Jewish. Likewise, a former member or sympathizer of the Gestapo could simply never talk about his or her past.[16] Either way, one could be reasonably certain that no incriminating photographs would suddenly appear, exposing one's family secret or lie. For most of the twentieth century, uncovering one's family history required advanced research skills, along with the money and time needed to visit archives and dig through reams of documents, often in unfamiliar languages, all without the aid of today's databases and search engines.

I discuss the experiences of the post–World War II generation here primarily as a point of contrast. After all, it is striking that many of the grandparents of today's children and teens—people born during and just following the war, in the 1940s and 1950s—were raised with an absence of childhood documentation. This absence of documentation led to theoretical work on the topics of memory and forgetting in the late twentieth and early twenty-first centuries.[17] It seems likely that the rise of memory studies in the social sciences and humanities would not have emerged if not for this absence and the related repression of memories that shaped the postwar period.[18] It is also not a coincidence that the field of memory studies has been driven largely by Jewish scholars grappling with the trauma of the Holocaust, and, albeit to a lesser extent, German scholars grappling with their families' and nation's silence over the atrocities they committed.[19]

A striking commonality among cultural theorists preoccupied with memory is that whatever side of history they happen to be on, their work is often based on the same premise: forgetting is memory's foe. Memory is sacred and forgetting is something to overcome. Memory is revered and forgetting is disparaged. In *Memory, History, Forgetting*, the philosopher Paul Ricoeur explores the relationship between memory and forgetting at length. As he observes, "On the whole, forgetting is experienced as an attack on the reliability of memory. An attack, a weakness, a lacuna. In this regard memory defines itself, at least in the first instance, as a struggle against forgetting."[20]

For all the disparagement of forgetting in contemporary cultural theorizing, at the same time, forgetting has also been a welcome panacea for a generation that longed to simply continue living.[21] One might say that during this period the future came to rely on forget-

ting, even as it was denounced. Some people even embraced forgetting as a form of survival. In *Testimony,* a book on witnessing and
memory after the Holocaust, the psychoanalyst Dori Laub and literary critic Shoshana Felman note that for those who chose not to
forget—for those who chose to remember and put their memories
into words—the cost was often life itself: "The act of telling might
itself become severely traumatizing. . . . Poets and writers who have
broken their silence may have indeed paid with their life for that deed
(Celan, Améry, Borowski, Levi, Bettleheim)."[22] Yet Laub and Felman
also recognize the complex ways in which forgetting affected other
writers of this generation, including former Nazi collaborators such
as the philosopher Paul de Man. Following de Man's death in 1983, a
researcher discovered over two hundred previously unknown articles
that he had written for Nazi collaborators in Belgium during World
War II. The discovery cast de Man's entire body of work into question. But if de Man chose to forget this period of his life and work, forgetting de Man may not be the only or correct response: "When we
cast de Man as 'Nazi' in a self-righteous bipartition of 'the good guys'
and 'the bad guys,' we profoundly *forget* what the Holocaust was like,
while at the same time we accuse de Man, precisely, of *forgetting,*
judging it unethical in his case. . . . In reality, we are all implicated—and
in more than one way—in de Man's forgetting, and in his silence."[23]

At issue is not whether one should forgive or overlook de Man's
hidden past but rather the dangers associated with oversimplifying
or establishing a hierarchy of forgetting. Simply put, in the twentieth century forgetting functioned as a crutch for a remarkably diverse range of people who hoped to stagger forward into the future.
That so many survivors managed to forget and subsequently never
pass along their memories to their children means that in some dys-
functional way, life did go on (albeit not without consequences). For

Germans and collaborators from other nations, like de Man, forgetting also facilitated some sort of return to normalcy. However, my point here is not that forgetting—the repression of memories of the Holocaust—is something to celebrate but rather that this collective erasure of the past was possible at all.

To appreciate just how remarkable it is that many of the grandparents of today's digitally connected children and youth were able to grow up and even grow old without fully confronting the past, consider how different the future will be for today's child and teen refugees and migrants. One of the most striking differences between earlier mass migrations and the current migration of people from Syria and parts of North Africa is the extent to which the crisis has been documented—and not simply by journalists. In the summers of 2015 and 2016, reporters told of migrants arriving on the shores of Greece and Italy with nothing but the clothes on their backs and small waterproof bags containing identification papers and mobile phones. These phones are now recognized as a necessity; in 2015, the United Nations High Commissioner for Refugees distributed 33,000 SIM cards to Syrian refugees in Jordan, along with 85,704 solar lanterns to be used for charging mobile phones.[24] These phones have already had a profound impact on the experiences of twenty-first-century migrants, who now record their journeys and the tragedies that happen along the way. The images are not only stored on their phones, but also circulate on Facebook and other social media platforms. There are selfies of migrants arriving in new locations—posted to let their family and friends know they have reached a destination safely—but also photographs of the atrocities encountered in transit. When today's young migrants are adults, will they—like an earlier generation of migrants—have the option of forgetting, or will their journeys lurk beside them for decades in the form of digital traces put into circulation by themselves and their fellow travelers? On the one hand, this evidence may mean that they will never have to engage in the difficult work of recovering repressed memories. On the other, one may ask: How will they forget just enough to move on and live a full and productive life in the present?

During and following World War II, many family members fell out of touch with each other—sometimes for years and sometimes for a lifetime. Today's migrants, in contrast, are often intimately linked to the family and friends they have left behind. When they leave, they take their networks with them. But this may have a downside. Those left behind may overwhelm the migrants with messages asking them for help or reminding them of the dire situation at home.[25] Moreover, how does one walk forward into the future carrying an archive of past images, some of harrowing events? What will the lives and futures of today's migrants be as a result? At stake here is the increasingly ambiguous status of photographs depicting conflict and migration. The media scholar Barbie Zelizer points out that most photos of the Holocaust, sometimes described as "atrocity photos," were documentary images that were typically public, not private documents. Today's migrants, while still the subject of documentary photographs, are also producing their own images, which often record intensely private moments yet end up on social media platforms where they are in turn reconfigured as public documents and as part of collective memories.[26]

Some evidence suggests that having one's past—no matter how traumatic—remain present may in fact ease one's transition into the future. Narrative exposure therapy, which is frequently used in work with young migrants and asylum seekers, treats symptoms of posttraumatic stress disorder by encouraging victims to narrate the key events in their lives. The premise is that by locating events, including traumatic events, on a timeline and describing them, the patients will be able to keep past traumas from overwhelming the future.[27] It is easy to imagine how a digital archive might assist in this task. However, these personal archives of photographs might not serve the same purpose if they continued to reappear uninvited, and out of context. What if child survivors of the Holocaust had grown up with constant access to photographs and films of the atrocities to which they bore witness as children? Would this have eased their suffering? Would such immediate and even relentless access to the past have enabled them to more easily grapple with the trauma of their childhoods? In a 1914 essay, Sigmund Freud distinguished remembering from repetition. To repeat something is not to remember it, he claimed, but rather to act out what has been forgotten: "The compulsion to repeat . . . replaces the impulsion to remember."[28] The role of the analyst is to break the endless cycle of repetition—to move the patient from repetition to remembering. The question is whether we will experience access to the past via personal digital archives of photographs and videos as a form of repetition or as a form of remembrance. Will the specific forms of repetition that arise in the absence of remembering cease to plague future generations? Or will a new set of challenges arise?

Anyone who has read Jorge Luis Borges's short fictions will recognize that an end to forgetting is bound to come with its own consequences and produce an entirely new set of maladies. In one of Borges's stories, a character named Ireneo Funes falls from his horse and hits his head, but when he wakes up from his unconscious state he has a new problem—the ability to remember everything in vivid detail. For Funes, "the present was almost intolerable in its richness and sharpness, as were his most distant and trivial memories." Funes disparagingly refers to his own memory as "a garbage heap."

Funes evidently had no reason to repeat the past in lieu of remembering it (after all, he remembered everything), but to suggest that his condition was liberating would be entirely misleading.[29] In "Funes the Memorious," as well as several of his other short fictions written long before digital archives began to restructure our daily lives, Borges appeared to foresee the risk of a past that can never be forgotten. But for children and youth, the consequences of carrying the past forward on such an unprecedented scale may be even greater than it is for adults.

The Value of Forgetting and Being Forgotten

Admittedly, most childhoods are not marked by the collective traumas described in the previous section. Despite their massive numbers, survivors and migrants remain minorities in the world. And even those whose childhoods are marked by extraordinary loss and violence often have at least a few memories they wish to carry forward into the future. Total and complete forgetting, then, is rarely something to which a person aspires, even if their childhood was far from perfect. Nevertheless, most people experience at least some events during childhood and adolescence that they would rather forget and have forgotten by others. For example, most people would prefer that the details recorded in their seventh-grade diary and the photographs published in their ninth-grade yearbook remain out of public circulation. The events and stages of life documented in these diaries and yearbooks may appear to be trivial, but even minor events often take on huge proportions for adolescents. Indeed, adolescents are especially prone to skewed or exaggerated perceptions of self. The exact content of one's ninth-grade yearbook photograph doesn't matter. What matters is that many adolescents experience even the smallest imperfections as insurmountable markers of inadequacy and sources of shame. Who wants or needs to repeat a shameful experience?

The fact that shameful and humiliating experiences are part and parcel of growing up may explain why childhood memories are, as Freud suggested, often molded by "powerful forces from a later period." What we remember is nothing more than scenes in which we are always the star. These are not true memories, but rather elaborations on childhood memories that have accrued all the baggage and censoring impulses of our later life experiences. "If the retained reminiscences of a person are subjected to an analytic test," wrote Freud, "it can be readily ascertained that a guarantee for their correctness does not exist. Some of the memory pictures are surely falsified and incomplete, or displaced in point of time and place."[30] So not only is much of our childhood forgotten or at least "concealed," but what we do remember is typically far from accurate.[31] Events are transposed into different contexts, people who never occupied the same place are brought together, and in some cases, objects come to stand in for entire periods of our life.

Freud's claims were based solely on observations recorded from the side of the analyst's couch, and they were subject to considerable criticism in the late twentieth century. But contemporary neuroscience is now lending support to at least some of his century-old claims about childhood and forgetting. This is not to suggest that we have yet arrived at a definitive definition of forgetting. Forgetting, like memory itself, continues to carry myriad definitions and explanations that vary not only across but often within disciplines. It is becoming increasingly apparent, however, that as much as forgetting can be unwanted, it does at times serve an important function.

In a 2014 study, the neuroscientists Donna Bridge and Joel Voss monitored participants' brains using an MRI scanner and found evidence that the brain "edits" memories. Memories were retained over time, but they were also continuously overwritten to remain relevant. The researchers maintain that the hippocampus, a region of the brain deeply entangled in autobiographical memory, plays an important role by allowing current information to affect memories of past experiences. They conclude that forgetting, at least partial forgetting, is pervasive and may hold a specific function. When the present "infiltrates" the past, it ensures that old memories remain relevant or worth carrying forward. At the same time, irrelevant or unpleasant information is deleted.[32]

So, whether one turns to psychoanalysis or neuroscience, the conclusions are similar: memories are far from accurate. They are always subject to some form of forgetting, or at least distortion. And the further back one goes, the more distorted one's memories become. One might assume that this is simply because childhood is more remote, but this doesn't explain why a sixty-year-old person's memories of their early twenties are generally far more accurate than a twenty-year-old person's memories of being seven or eight. Freud suggested that childhood reminiscences, which he also described as "concealing memories" and "screen memories," have more in common with "the legends and myths of nations" than with the memories of one's later years.[33] In other words, more than accurate recollections of specific events, childhood memories are stories called upon from time to time to make sense of irrecoverable yet significant moments. But a series of questions remains: Why is childhood forgetting so prevalent? What is the purpose of remembering only particular scenes that are selectively restaged over the years?[34]

The purpose of both legends and myths is to explain otherwise inexplicable phenomena. If our childhood memories fall into these categories, perhaps it is because growing up itself is a difficult and mysterious process that can only be fully understood by resorting to mythology. Legends and myths circulate in the absence of empirical evidence, though legends are often grounded in partial facts (evidential enough to hold the appearance of the real but not evidential enough to be reflections of the real). But what happens when the ability to magically turn our youth into legends and myths is usurped? What happens when we can no longer find a way to become the heroes of these self-made tales? What happens when our memories of childhood are no longer primarily based on stories that have the appearance of reality but rather on documentary evidence, such as photographs and videos of our childhood in circulation online?

Perhaps even more important than the ability to forget is the ability to be forgotten by others. If it matters that other people—our future friends, employers, lovers, and children—never encounter who we were before we matured, it is because maturation is as much an accumulation of knowledge as it is an accumulation of forgetting. Indeed, maturation has historically been about "moving on" and, in the process, achieving a distance from the many embarrassing and awkward events that punctuate childhood and adolescence. Historically, elaborate rituals marked a young person's passage into the adult world. In some of these rituals, forgetting was even part of the process. In his 1909 book *The Rites of Passage,* the anthropologist Arnold van Gennep observed that initiation rites frequently require the initiate to "die" or act dead (typically, hallucinogens, such as peyote, as well as flagellation or other violent means are used to accomplish this task). The goal is "to make [the initiate] forget his former personality and his former world."[35] Underpinning these initiation rituals is an assumption that entry into adulthood requires a complete departure from childhood—a radical rupture realized by effectively forgetting the past.

This brings us back to the rather commonplace problem presented at the beginning of this chapter—the dilemma facing today's youth, who are no longer able to easily destroy those traces of the past with which they no longer wish to live. But the problem is not simply that we can no longer clandestinely destroy embarrassing photographs. The shift from analogue to digital is affecting our experience of the past on at least three important levels. First, there are now more images of young people in circulation than ever before. Second, for the first time, these images are predominantly taken by children and teens themselves. Finally, a unique aspect of our current era is the ability to preserve not only images of the past but also the social networks affiliated with these images. A photograph posted online is usually linked to an entire social network of people both familiar and unknown. What today's youth will carry forward into the future, then, is not simply an archive of digital images and video clips but an entire social context that they may or may not wish to retain. It is on this basis that the European Commission drafted legislation proposing that "data subjects" should have the right to obtain the erasure of personal data relating to themselves, especially data produced when they were children.[36]

My goal in this book is not to argue that digital media are bound to harm children. Nearly every new media technology has resulted in a moral panic about potential harms, and this reaction almost always rests on false assumptions about children's innocence. Nor do I make a case for curtailing young people's access to digital media. Rather, my intent is to explore what may be at stake as we enter an era when the ability to detach ourselves from childhood and adolescence—and to edit our childhood memories—appears to be profoundly at risk. What we are now facing is the prospect of having documentation of our youthful lives broadcast on what may best be described as a continuous loop. And unlike a printed high school yearbook, a personal photo album, or a shoebox full of memorabilia, the information that accumulates on social media platforms is also part of other people's collections. Traces of the past are now networked, linked, and never fully in our control. This means that social networks forged during our early years are likely to remain in place throughout our adult life.

What we are facing is not simply a shift from private to shared memorabilia and from memorabilia that we can easily destroy with our bare hands to memorabilia that are entirely out of our hands, but also the arrival of a world where the ability to break away from the past is severely compromised and may even be controlled by private interests invested in keeping our past networks intact. If we were once able to edit or "overwrite" our childhood memories in order to carry forward only information deemed relevant or tolerable, we are now entering an era in which our relationship to the past is out of our control. Our private photo albums—and to the extent that they can be translated into data, our private relationships, gestures, and even desires—increasingly belong to others. The consequences, which are only beginning to become visible, are bound to have a profound impact on what it means to grow up and leave home in the twenty-first century.

1 Documenting Childhood before and after Social Media

C hildhood has been recorded and preserved in a variety of mediums for centuries—from portraits of seventeenth-century aristocrats, to family snapshots, to home movies shot on film or video. With each era's new imaging technologies, childhood has been subjected to different types of documentation with different consequences. Early portraits often sought to symbolically locate children within a broader social or political context, and the very earliest photographs of children nearly always presented them in the isolated confines of a photographer's studio; but as more quotidian forms of image-making emerged, children's lives became increasingly exposed. As photography moved out of the studio and into the hands of the people, even children's messes and tears could be documented. With the advent of portable photography, children were able to represent themselves from their own perspective for the first time. Each of these transitions was significant, but the digital era stands out from these earlier periods of image-making on several accounts.

In the past, children and even adolescents had only limited means to document their experiences of growing up, for several reasons. First, the available technologies were often monitored by adults and, due to cost, were not very accessible to the average child or teen. Second, earlier media technologies, from portable roll-film cameras to camcorders, were used to record events (e.g., school concerts, birthday parties, and graduations) but not, again due to cost, everyday life as it unfolded. Much of what is captured in today's selfies simply did not exist in the era of analogue photography. Finally, while people sometimes made duplicates of photographs to share with grandparents or friends, personal photographs nearly always remained singular, not plural. They were made for preservation in a private context (e.g., a family album) rather than for widespread sharing. The same held true for home movies. Whether shot on film or video, most home movies were one-of-a-kind artifacts. With the introduction of digital photography and video, the convergence of the camera with the mobile phone, and the development of social media platforms, these restrictions have largely dissolved. Digital media and social media platforms have profoundly changed the production, content, and number of images in circulation, as well as the potential audience for these images in the present and the future.

Representing Children and Childhood before Photography

Even before childhood was widely recognized as a concept, children were represented in art. These representations can be found on ancient urns and woven into medieval tapestries. However, representations of childhood scenes themselves were rare. It was not until the late sixteenth century that painters began to approach children and childhood as subjects, and even then, only fleetingly.[1]

In Annibale Carracci's *Two Children Teasing a Cat* (1587–1588), for example, the viewer encounters a scene that appears to offer a rare glimpse into childhood in the sixteenth century. In the painting, a young girl watches as a somewhat older boy taunts an orange cat with a crayfish. A portrait neither of a single child nor of children posing with their family, *Two Children Teasing a Cat* stands out as a rare representation of children living in a children's world. There is play, a pet, and most notably, not an adult in sight.

More common in the late sixteenth to mid-seventeenth centuries were family portraits in which children slipped into the background, sometimes assuming even less importance than the objects included to foreground the intellectual interests of the family's patriarch.[2] This is demonstrated in Charles Le Brun's large-scale 1660 family portrait, *Everhard Jabach (1618–1695) and His Family.* In the painting, Jabach's four children appear to play a secondary role to Jabach's impressive collection of objects, which includes books, drawings, ancient busts, and a celestial globe. But the children in Le Brun's portrait of the Jabach clan are clearly portrayed as children—that is, their attire and location in the private home suggest they are living a somewhat sheltered existence. In many other European paintings from the period, however, children are still depicted as miniature adults. This is not entirely surprising, since the concept of childhood did not emerge in all classes at the same time in Europe.[3] In Jean Michelin's 1656 painting *The Baker's Cart,* a baker, standing next to his cart of bread, is flanked by an older woman peddling goods and another adult male, as well as four children. Here, the distinction between the children and the adults is indicated only by height. In attire, activity, and expression, the children are barely distinguishable from the adults and seem to have no special place or role in the world.

By the eighteenth century and into the early nineteenth century, European painters began to embrace childhood as a subject more frequently. The eighteenth-century French painter Jean Siméon Chardin, for example, depicted children engaged in activities that remain common to this day. *Boy Building a House of Cards* (1730s) shows a young boy playing alone with a deck of cards. In one of the four existing versions of this painting, the young boy is shown wearing an apron—a detail presumably added to point to his status as a servant. The inclusion of both aristocratic and working-class children in Chardin's *Boy Building a House of Cards* series points to a rising consciousness and growing concern about childhood and its special status as a time of life distinct from adulthood. Of course, even in the nearly documentary perspective on childhood offered by Chardin, the viewer's access to childhood is entirely framed by the adult gaze of the painter.

It should not come as a surprise that children were not able to represent themselves in the sixteenth to eighteen centuries. Self-representation was also new to adults during this period. With the invention of movable type, literacy rates soared, and the primarily oral societies of the Middle Ages, which valued collective and communal activities, gave way to more private and individualistic societies where the individual subject gained heightened status. Among other consequences, this led to the appearance of myriad new genres of writing, including the essay and the diary.[4] But if adults, at least a certain class of adults, discovered the freedom to explore their own interiority through writing and reading, the effects of early print culture were much more profound for children.

Many historians have suggested that a division between the cultures of adults and children was one of the many far-reaching consequences of the invention of movable type.[5] But it would be wrong to conclude that the only way in which print affected children was by exiling them from the world of adults. As children increasingly slipped outside the adult world to which they had once belonged, new kinds of books appeared with the primary intent of regulating what children should learn, do, and even think. From the fifteenth through the eighteenth centuries, pedagogical guides, parenting books, and conduct manuals were among the most popular books in circulation. Guides offering advice on how to rear and teach children were the bread and butter of many early publishers. Of course, children were the subjects, not the authors, of these texts. Thus, while childhood was only rarely taken up as a subject by painters in this period, it was given full and even excessive attention in print. There were educational tracts, parenting guides, primers, conduct books, domestic manuals, and catechisms. Approaching the child like a piece of machinery—an assemblage of separate parts each requiring special attention—manuals offered guidelines on how to keep everything about the child in working order. Educational tracts and pedagogical guides targeted the child's mind, parenting guides and domestic manuals targeted the child's physical and social well-being, and conduct books and catechisms sought to regulate the child's moral development. No part of the child was untouched. This trend would later lead Michel Foucault to categorize children alongside patients, madmen, and prisoners as subjects of excessive documentation and yet also as subjects relegated to silence. "This turning of real lives into writing," Foucault wrote, functioned "as a procedure of objectification and subjection." It was in this context that schools were established where instruction was carried out "with few words, no explanation, a total silence only interrupted by signals."[6]

For the first four centuries after the invention of childhood, children remained eerily silent. They were seen, occasionally represented through the eyes of adults in art, and explored as subjects in myriad discourses (pedagogical, moral, and medical), but they were rarely heard or permitted to represent themselves. Writing with light—photography—would finally bring childhood out of the dark corners to which it had been confined and, more importantly, it would give children the tools needed to engage in self-representation.

Children and Childhood in the Age of Photography

Even though children and childhood were increasingly depicted in paintings during the eighteenth century, children themselves still had limited means to represent their lives. This largely reflects the fact that while children probably did depict themselves in their own sketches and doodles, painting a portrait was a skill that took years to master. Simply put, because children were never master painters, self-representations of childhood from a prephotographic age were rare. With photography, however, children were finally able to represent their own lives. Over time, photographs would come to play an integral role in documenting childhood and would even drive the development of new photographic technologies. But this shift was by no means immediate. It would take nearly a century to achieve.

Although experiments with camera obscura date back to antiquity, the invention of photography is most often situated in the early nineteenth century, when several experiments and subsequent patents appeared simultaneously in France and England. The fierce competition that drove the early development of photography helped to quickly transform this new image-making medium from a mysterious process to one with a growing commercial application and market. By the 1840s, commercial photography was already well established in many European cities. In 1847, over two hundred cameras and an estimated half million plates were sold in Paris alone. As patents for specific developing processes were further relaxed in the 1850s, photography continued to gain ground as a medium of and for the people. By 1861, over 33,000 Parisians claimed to make their living from photography and its allied trades.[7]

The development of photography into a major industry in Europe had much to do with the popularity of portrait photography. While portrait painting remained out of reach to all but the most privileged families, with photography, portraiture became increasingly accessible. By the mid-nineteenth century, even modest working-class families could afford to acquire at least one family portrait. As the century progressed, there was also no need to live in or visit a major city to access portraiture services. By the 1860s, many small villages already had photography studios, and traveling vans brought the photography studio to even the most isolated outposts.[8]

It should not come as a surprise that children, either on their own or with their parents, were among the most popular subjects of early portrait photographers. By the time photography emerged, the idea of childhood had firmly taken root in Western cultures, and children had become popular objects both of inquiry (for everyone from medical doctors to pedagogues) and of adoration. Photography offered adults a way to more closely study children (with the aid of a camera, one could observe phenomena not readily visible to the human eye) and to celebrate and even preserve this now venerated stage of life.

This preoccupation with children and childhood, combined with the relative accessibility of the medium of photography, meant that few children would successfully dodge the photographer's lens by the end of the nineteenth century, and nearly none would do so by the end of the twentieth.[9] Indeed, by the time Kodak started to publish its trade magazine *Kodakery* in 1916, photography of children had been firmly established. *Kodakery*'s pages are replete with photographs of babies and children. As is the case in contemporary forms of advertising, these photographs often accompanied promotions that had no obvious connection to babies or children. The magazine also regularly featured child-related photography tips, such as how best to photograph fidgety young children, and how to create memory albums that children could enjoy as they grew older.[10]

By the time *Kodakery* went into circulation, however, something else had shifted in the world of photography: the ability to take photographs became accessible to children themselves. For most of the nineteenth century, children remained as silent as they had been in the era of painting and print. This was due to two technical restrictions. First, cameras were large, heavy, and complicated, which made them difficult, if not impossible, for a small child to operate. Second, before the invention of roll film, photographers had to develop the film themselves and do so very quickly. Photographic plates had to be developed nearly immediately after a photograph was taken or the image would be permanently lost. Given the knowledge, skill, and speed required to develop photographs, few nineteenth-century children ever had an opportunity to engage in their own image-making.

Two technological developments had a permanent impact on photography and on children's ability to represent their own lives. By the late nineteenth century, the first compact cameras, which were light, user-friendly, and portable, had appeared. Even more important was the invention of roll film in the late 1890s. With roll film, which would come to dominate photography for nearly a century thereafter, anyone could now take photographs and outsource the development. To capitalize on this new, simpler, and safer process, the entrepreneur George Eastman also did something that would have a significant impact on children's ability to represent their own lives and childhood itself: he invented a camera designed just for young people.

A Media Technology Made Just for Children

With the arrival of the Brownie camera, photography transformed from an image-making medium reserved for professionals and serious amateurs to one that was widely accessible. Eastman ingeniously chose to adopt the name Brownie from a popular Victorian-era children's book series, *The Brownies,* by Palmer Cox, which featured the antics of mischievous little cartoon figures called Brownies. As Todd Gustavson, the technology curator at George Eastman House, observes, "Cox's Brownies scampering over the camera's carton and ads made sure children would know Brownie was made for them." Every Brownie camera also came with a fifty-four-page booklet offering photography tips and inviting new owners to join the Brownie Camera Club. The camera, developed largely as a toy, was relatively affordable, costing only $2 (roughly equivalent to $60 today). Largely due to their low price, Brownies would end up gaining popularity with many new adult photographers, but the camera was primarily marketed as a starter camera for future photographers.[11] The Brownie stands as an early example of building brand loyalty by enticing the very youngest consumers.

The introduction of the Brownie did two things that a media technology had never done before. The Brownie gave children the ability to represent their own world from their own perspective by turning cameras into toys and photography into play. And it demonstrated the development of a new technology that was driven by the needs and desires of children rather than adults.

Before the invention of the Brownie, new media technologies, from the printing press to the telegraph to the typewriter, had responded to the needs of adults and were developed to facilitate work, not play. Eastman understood the value of paying attention to the needs of amateurs and children and of focusing on play rather than work.[12] The significance of Eastman's insights and his decision to act on these insights is apparent when we realize that following the Brownie, children and youth would not play a major role in the development of a new media technology until the 1970s. It was at this time that Atari started to develop games with young consumers in mind. By the late 1970s, Atari had also launched a home computer division with a mandate to produce affordable, child-friendly computers capable of competing with the computers then coming on the market from Apple. Steve Jobs, who cofounded Apple in 1976, had previously been a successful game developer at Atari, and he had evidently taken a page from the company's insights into the value of developing technologies for the average consumer—including the very young consumer—rather than for business executives. Today, much of Jobs's legacy rests on his decision to pursue this business model, but on this account, the credit given to him may be displaced. The history of the Brownie suggests that George Eastman recognized the value of developing technologies for the average consumer over half a century before Jobs was even born.[13]

The Brownie would remain on the market for over seventy years. In the first decade of the camera's existence, Kodak issued more than fifty different models in an effort to refine its prototype and appeal to an ever-expanding market.[14] Over the next forty years, nearly two hundred more models would reach the market. During this time childhood would also increasingly come to be experienced through photography, and Kodak appeared to be fully aware of the fact that its affordable and portable cameras were playing a role in this transformation. In a 1923 issue of *Kodakery,* one commentator, philosophically reflecting on our ability to remember childhood, wrote, "Kodak is a partner of Memory—a silent partner, yet able to be very eloquent, full of interesting suggestions without saying a word."[15] In another 1923 issue, Kodak cameras were promoted as a remedy not only for the problem of forgetting but also for the tendency of human memory to exaggerate traumatic past events. "I was born before there were any Kodaks," the author of the piece laments. "And I've been wishing I had a picture of my funny self on the day I first went to school in that little red brick school house with my lunch in a queer tin pail. I have the memory, and it is fearfully dramatic. But I'd like to have the picture." With the aid of photographs, the writer mused, it is easier not only to remember the past but also to avoid the "tricks" of memory that so often exaggerate or blur personal memories: "There is a pleasant trick about memory that it shows the happy moments very sharply and the unpleasant moments blurred a good deal."[16] The message is clear: with one's Kodak, it is possible to avoid repressing unhappy moments and conversely, to avoid remembering minor events as being more dramatic or important than they were in reality. The Kodak, then, was marketed as both an aid to memory and an important corrective—a way to preempt remembering childhood through what Freud had described only a decade earlier as "screen memories," or displaced memories that effectively conceal or distort events from one's childhood, especially traumatic events.[17]

In this respect, the Brownie and other affordable and user-friendly cameras affected childhood on two levels. To the extent that the Brownie helped to popularize photography for children and adults alike, childhood became increasingly well documented. As a result, childhood also came to be remembered and understood through photographs. More important, the Brownie offered children a viable way to engage in self-representation for the first time. Yet the Brownie was not without its own built-in restrictions.

Many people had the means to purchase a Brownie (indeed, hundreds of thousands of children in the early to mid-twentieth century grew up with this model of camera), but throughout the Brownie's reign, the cost of film and developing remained an obstacle. In the early years of the Brownie, camera film sold for 15 cents a roll, and each roll offered only six exposures.[18] While 15 cents may appear minimal, in 1910, some American workers still made less than 20 cents per hour, and even unionized skilled tradespeople rarely made over 50 cents per hour.[19] The cost of just twelve photographs could exceed an adult laborer's hourly wage. For most children, then, the idea of snapping twenty or more photographs per day—a practice that is now commonplace—would have been inconceivable. But this was not the only restriction associated with the Brownie and other twentieth-century roll-film cameras.

In the world of analogue photography, what one could represent was also subject to restrictions. One consideration was cost—the photographer had to decide what was memorable enough to be worth the price of development. Censorship was another consideration.

Anyone who did not own a camera that came with its own developing dish and printing materials, or who did not belong a photography club and have coveted access to a darkroom, would have been forced to take their film to a local photography shop for developing.[20] Most people gave little thought to the staff who worked in photography shops or in the lonely Fotomat booths that eventually came to dot shopping mall parking lots across North America in the 1960s to 1980s. But the people who worked in these shops and in their off-site developing laboratories did view and sometimes censor photographs. In 1986, the *Chicago Tribune* published a short article about Nancy Unger, one of the many invisible sets of eyes who worked the nightshift at a massive Fotomat processing plant in Addison, Illinois. Among the endless landscapes and birthday parties, Unger reported seeing thousands of dead bodies in coffins, pairs of buttocks, and even carefully staged home pornography scenes. In Unger's words, "In this job you realize how many weird people there really are."[21] While Fotomat, like most developers, had a relatively liberal policy about developing even the most lascivious photographs, it was bound by law to report any pornography involving children. For teens, the law posed a challenge. While adults could generally get away with producing their own naughty selfies, similar photographs snapped by teens of themselves or each other would have been flagged as potential forms of child pornography.[22] In addition to the prying eyes of parents, then, in the analogue era, children's and teens' self-representations were generally subject to both external and self-imposed censorship. There was, however, one photographic technology that offered something that approximated the degree of freedom now experienced with digital camera phones—the Polaroid.

Youth Culture and the Polaroid

If there is a technology that anticipated at least some of the potential image-making activities of the twenty-first century camera phone, it was not the Brownie but the Polaroid—more specifically, the Polaroid Swinger. Although instant cameras were first introduced in the 1940s, it was not until the mid-1960s that Edwin Land developed and marketed an affordable version of his Land Camera.[23] Like the Brownie, Land's instant camera was designed first and foremost for young photographers. However, unlike the Brownie, it was marketed chiefly to teenagers rather than children.[24] Land evidently understood that this demographic represented not only a sizable part of the population—largely due to the post–World War II baby boom—but also an easily influenced group of consumers. As a result, when he started to produce a mass-market version of his instant camera, he built it with teen needs and desires in mind. Provocatively called the Swinger, the camera was fun, affordable, and heavily promoted in teen-focused magazines, such as *American Girl,* and during advertisements that interrupted popular 1960s programs like *Batman* and *Lost in Space.* But as the film historian Peter Buse observes, in the case of Polaroid cameras, young people were not only central to the camera's promotion, but were also "taken to be the most natural participants in instant, integral photography, credited with understanding it spontaneously, instinctively."[25] If there is any doubt about Buse's claim that teens possess an inherent affinity for Polaroid technology, one need only consider that even in the age of digital camera phones, Polaroid photography persists. While certainly not the most common form of image-making today, Polaroid photography remains a popular pastime for tweens and teens. (Urban Outfitters, a clothing store that targets tweens, teens, and young adults, has a section dedicated to the sale of Polaroid cameras, film, and accessories.) But what is it about the Polaroid that has long appealed to young photographers?

There are at least two features of the Polaroid that the Brownie and other roll-film cameras never offered. First, the Polaroid reflected the temporality of the average tween or teen photographer. Because the film did not have to be sent out for development, it was possible to enjoy Polaroid images almost instantly. In the 1970s, Polaroid Swinger advertisements underscored the camera's rapid output by depicting young people taking and immediately sharing their photographs. They rarely showed anyone preserving photographs for posterity. In the 1990s, advertisements for the Polaroid Joycam went a step further, depicting teens sharing Polaroid images in a swimming pool—a location that represents the very counterpoint to preservation.[26] The message Polaroid conveyed was that their instant photographs were meant for pleasure in the present but not necessarily for the preservation of memories. This was remarkably different from Kodak, which marketed its affordable cameras as memory-making machines.

The other important way in which the Polaroid camera stood apart from earlier image-making technologies was the extent to which it effectively bypassed the censorship of both parents and film developers. If deviant photography had once required access to a darkroom and at least a basic knowledge of developing processes, with the Polaroid, such access and knowledge was no longer required. With this new instant image-making "toy," tweens and teens could snap a picture of their genitals or photograph friends smoking up behind their high school and be reasonably assured that they would get away with it.[27] While such uses of Polaroid cameras were not necessarily widespread, at least part of the technology's appeal was its ability to circumvent the prying eyes of adults—whether they belonged to one's parents or to workers developing film at a processing plant hundreds of miles away.[28]

In providing a way to bypass adult gatekeeping, the Polaroid camera brought image-making as close to the current era of photography as it would get in the analogue era. Young people were finally free to represent aspects of childhood and youth culture that had previously been carefully redacted (either preemptively by young people themselves or by adult censors). On this basis, Buse suggests that Polaroid cameras, despite their differences from camera phones, have informed how camera phones are now used.[29] What separates tweens' and teens' engagement with Polaroid photography from digital camera-phone photography, however, are two factors that cannot be overlooked: cost and the potential for duplication and wide-scale circulation. While Polaroid cameras were affordable (when launched, they retailed for less than $20 and were considered in reach for at least 70 percent of American families), the cost of Polaroid film was always comparatively high.[30] The other and more notable difference between Polaroid image-making and digital photography is connected to the Polaroid photograph's limited ability to be duplicated and shared. Ultimately, a Polaroid image is a one-of-a-kind document that has more in common with unique works of art than with products reflecting the qualities of mechanical or digital reproduction. Consequently, while the practice of taking Polaroid photographs may be similar to that of taking digital images, the result is remarkably different. Polaroid images circulate as ephemeral, intimate, and singular prints that are quite distinct from digital images, with their reproducibility and mobility.

Although Polaroid images are not highly reproducible, that does not mean that they cannot be preserved. The widespread belief that these images tend to fade over time is largely a myth. If not exposed to direct sunlight, Polaroid images are just as enduring as most film-based photographic formats. This myth probably reflects the way these images have generally circulated. Frequently put on immediate display, Polaroid images often ended up tacked to a bulletin board or taped to a wall instead of being put in a photo album. If the format has subsequently gained a reputation for fading over time and in the process failing to augment our long-term memories, it likely reflects how people have chosen to engage with Polaroid images.

Home Movies from Celluloid to Video

Alongside photography, the twentieth century was profoundly shaped by at least two other technologies that would eventually seep into the private sphere: film and video. Although film and video technologies did not spread as widely as still photography due to cost and the technical skills needed to operate the cameras, from the late 1920s onward, home moviemaking technologies nevertheless changed how childhood and adolescence were experienced and recorded. This is undoubtedly why in the twenty-first century, the gritty and faded aesthetic of home movies has become the hallmark of what it meant to grow up in an era before digital technologies. Artists now flock to flea markets in search of abandoned film footage, and around the world, lost-film archives, many largely made up of home movies, have emerged to preserve at least some of the works of twentieth-century do-it-yourself filmmakers.[31] Even mainstream directors frequently splice old home movie footage (or footage shot to look like old home movie footage) into their films as a provocative substitute for memory. As if memory itself were equipped with era-specific filters, it is now common for film characters to remember the 1970s in flashbacks that appear to have been shot on Super 8 film, and to remember the 1980s via aging video clips.[32] Despite this common trope in contemporary film, in the twentieth century, home movies were not primarily embraced as technologies of memory.

By the 1920s, Kodak was already marketing its first line of Ciné-Kodak products to families with the financial means to buy in to the home moviemaking craze. As the film studies scholar Patricia Zimmermann writes, home movies did circulate as "cinema of memory," offering "empirical evidence of otherwise lost events," but they also functioned as "political interventions, dreamscapes, and phantasms." Amateur films were frequently the only form of moving-image documentation available, especially in minority communities, but this does not mean they were purely documentary. These films often served multiple functions and were informed by complex personal and collective investments and desires.[33] They were promoted and embraced both as technologies of documentation and preservation and as ways for amateur filmmakers to imagine and create possible worlds.

While it is true that movie cameras were sometimes marketed as a way to preserve family memories, from the time they were launched in the 1920s, they were also promoted for creative uses. A 1928 promotional brochure for the Ciné-Kodak, for example, offered detailed instructions not only on how to shoot a wedding party and a child taking their very first steps, but also on how to shoot a fictional film. Indeed, families that purchased the Ciné-Kodak were encouraged to also purchase a copy of Kodak's 132-page booklet "Junior Scenarios for Home Movies," which explained how to turn fairy tales into films starring one's own family members. From a "playlet" of seven scenes to a "super-production" of 122 scenes, the manual walked Ciné-Kodak owners through the process of casting and preparing young actors and staging, shooting, and editing their own film.[34] Kodak recognized early on that its moving-image cameras were also technologies that might spark users' imaginations and enable them to create other worlds and scenarios.

Evidence of the widespread use of early home film cameras for imaginative rather than simply documentary purposes is well documented in back issues of *Movie Maker*, a magazine for amateur filmmakers produced by the Amateur Cinema League, which was established in 1926. The first issue of *Amateur Movie Maker* included a report on what it hailed as the "first amateur motion picture production." *Love by Proxy*, the magazine explained, was produced by "some twenty youngsters, just out of high school," and led by Eugene W. Ragsdale, a New Jersey teenager who had "been playing with a camera since he was knee high to a grasshopper."[35] Until video camcorders became widely available, however, moviemaking among children and teens was uncommon. More often than not, amateur moviemaking placed young people in front of the camera, either as documentary subjects or as actors, rather than behind the camera.

Technically finicky and relatively expensive, most early amateur filmmakers were male heads of household.[36] On the surface, the home movie phenomenon appears to have been driven by a desire to celebrate children. A 1929 article on home movies in *Parents Magazine* noted, "The love of parents for their children is the most important factor in the present rapid accelerating popularity of home movies."[37] Home movie technologies were designed for parents rather than children, according to Zimmermann, who observes that "with their reels and projectors, they could prolong the duration of the prototypical nuclear family."[38] However, there is at least some evidence suggesting that the reasons for making home films stretched beyond a documentary impulse. A passage in the second issue of *Amateur Movie Maker,* published in 1927, suggested that although some male heads of household embraced amateur moviemaking as a way to preserve their perfect family, others might have been motivated by a wish to re-imagine their families: "What a movie-amateur actually has in his hand is a machine for inventing himself. He can even invent his own children (after he gets them started)—make them over the way he wants them, or just give the movies to his children and before he knows it they will begin making over themselves."[39] This curious passage is further evidence that if photography was "a partner of Memory—a silent partner," the home movie camera served another purpose. In addition to functioning as memory machines, home movie camera technologies could serve as silent partners in fantasy and desire.

The filmmaker Zoe Beloff, who frequently mines old home film footage in her work, explains, "For a great many years, I have thought of the home movie in the same way that Freud thought of dreams, jokes, and slips of the tongue—that is, as revealing more than the amateur filmmakers ever intended." Beloff notes that in her *Dream Film* series, which is entirely composed of found home movie footage, she sought to bring to the surface "repressed desires and daily traumas that are visible in all home movies if we know how to read them."[40] Beloff's understanding of home movies as spaces in which social actors—in this case, family members—play out repressed desires and traumas suggests that if home movies are to be approached as spaces of memory, they may best be viewed as documents that conceal or displace as much as they expose.

If filmmakers like Beloff are now able to exploit the double life of the home movie, it has much to do with the fact that from the 1920s to the 1970s, home moviemaking technologies became increasingly accessible, enabling a widening spectrum of families to make home movies. By the 1950s, even many lower-middle-class families owned movie cameras and projection equipment.[41] Still, throughout this period, the cost of buying and developing film was out of reach for the average child or teen. And unlike with still cameras, no significant attempts were ever made to market movie cameras exclusively to young people. This did not change until the arrival of video.

Although home video dates back to the 1970s, it was largely inaccessible to the average family for more than a decade. In 1983, Sony's first camcorder for domestic use retailed at $1,500. Two years later, prices started to rapidly decline. By 1985, a budding amateur filmmaker could purchase an Amstrad VMC100 for just $400. Videocassettes were available for just a few dollars and could even be reused.[42] The relatively low cost of the equipment, the ability to shoot on new or recycled videocassettes, and the elimination of the developing process meant that one could now shoot for longer periods of time, afford to be considerably more reckless about what to shoot, and do so with little outside surveillance. Since video recording, unlike most home film formats, had sound-recording capabilities, the medium also naturally promoted new types of home movies, such as oral histories. Editing videos was also easier than editing film; it could be executed, not without considerable patience, by anyone with access to a television monitor and a VCR. Yet many home videos were never edited. Because it was possible to immediately play back the footage one had just shot either on the camera itself or with the aid of a VCR and monitor, many people watched recorded events as the events were still unfolding. At a birthday party, for example, someone might record a child blowing out the candles on a cake and then instantly replay the scene for partygoers.

It was in this context that male heads of household were finally displaced as the primary home moviemakers. By the end of the 1980s, it was commonplace for middle and high school students to dabble in moviemaking, both for school projects and for pleasure. Children and teens could make their own educational videos and also engage in more imaginative activities. Indeed, in the 1980s and 1990s, people used home video cameras for an entire range of moviemaking activities, from recording stupid backyard stunts to video-based versions of fan fiction and amateur pornography.[43]

Just as the Polaroid camera gave children and teens increased control over the types of images they produced, so home video cameras offered them control over moving images. In the late 1980s, there was even a short-lived attempt to turn video cameras into toys. In 1987, Fisher-Price released its model PXL-2000 toy camcorder, which recorded highly pixilated black-and-white moving images. Among other qualities, the PXL-2000 was exceptionally small and light, and, unlike any other video camera, it recorded moving images on inexpensive and widely available audiocassettes. Although the PXL-2000 was only produced for a year (at first retailing for just under $200 and then for a still pricey but more accessible $100), its short existence exposed the possibilities of putting video cameras into the hands of young moviemakers.[44] With the arrival of video, teens' lives and modes of self-representation entered a new era. This is demonstrated in the artist Sadie Benning's 1989 film, *Me & Rubyfruit,* which was shot on a PXL-2000 that Benning had received as a gift when she was fifteen. Made in the privacy of her bedroom, the film offered an unprecedented glimpse into adolescent lesbian desire. With text culled from Rita Mae Brown's 1973 lesbian novel *Rubyfruit Jungle* and images from porn magazines and phone sex advertisements, the film, even decades later, remains a provocative exploration of queer adolescent sexuality, desire, and longing.[45] That anyone saw Benning's film at all, however, likely had less to do with the video medium than with the fact that the filmmaker's father, who gave her the camera, was himself a filmmaker. Benning was already familiar with the independent film festival circuit in her teens and had the connections needed to secure screenings. Any teen without such connections would have found it extremely challenging to circulate their independent video productions in the late 1980s.

For all of video technology's democratizing potential, it did not offer a platform for circulation. One could make a copy of a video and share it with friends, but even the most widely circulated home video productions would reach an audience no larger than that of the average photocopied zine. Like zines, which typically are produced in print runs of only twenty-five to fifty, home videos remained limited-edition items. They were not one-of-a-kind, like Polaroid photographs, but reproducibility was never a hallmark of home video. What few people predicted in the 1980s, however, was that video recordings would also turn out to be highly ephemeral. Beyond the fact that both Betamax and VHS formats would become nearly obsolete when digital formats, such as DAT and DVD, gained popularity, videocassettes would also prove vulnerable to various forms of environmental exposure. Betamax and VHS tapes are among the most fragile media formats in existence. Without proper storage or transfer to a more stable format, many videos shot in the 1980s and 1990s will not survive into the 2030s. But for those who grew up in the age of video, the medium's fragility may offer a welcome reprieve from the past. While many embarrassing home videos from the 1980s and 1990s still exist, few of them are still viewable, even if one does have access to a VCR in the corresponding format.

Documenting Childhood and Adolescence
in the Era of Social Media

Children and adolescents have long been favorite subjects for artistic representation. With the advent of photography they were finally able, albeit with certain restrictions, to take representation into their own hands. Today, with the combination of digital media and social media platforms, we are in a new and arguably unprecedented era of image-making that has specific consequences for youth. Since the early 2000s, the content, scale, and context of personal photography and home moviemaking have changed, and in the process, young people have come to play greater roles in both practices.

Even in the later period of analogue photography, the content of photographs still reflected a relatively high degree of selectivity (because every photograph came at a cost) and censorship (because of monitoring by adults). Unless one had access to a darkroom, a third party had to be involved in the developing process. Although Polaroid technologies put developing into the photographer's own hands, the resulting images could not be reproduced. The photographs that young people created in the analogue era were remarkably different from much of today's digital content. Bluntly put, in the age of the Fotomat, a teenager hoping to engage in the analogue equivalent to sexting would have first had to risk taking the film to a clerk working at the local photography store, cross their fingers that whoever was working at the developing plant was too exhausted to notice the questionable content on the roll of film, and then find a covert way to send the photograph to its intended recipient. While a small number of teens certainly managed to circumvent such obstacles, there was no widespread equivalent to today's sexting. In other words, while the age of roll-film and Polaroid photography was by no means innocent, neither technology managed to generate the type of content that is possible in the digital era. But content isn't the only thing that has changed.

The number of photographs and videos shot every day has sky-rocketed, largely because image- and video-production is now essentially free. Once one has a smartphone—and in many places in the world, even elementary school students do—the cost of producing and circulating images is negligible. In 2000, a mere 80 billion photographs were shot around the world. By 2015, this number had increased to over one trillion, with 75 percent of them shot on a mobile phone.[46] While it is impossible to determine the exact percentage of photographs shot by people under the age of eighteen, there are compelling reasons to believe that child and adolescent photographers are disproportionately represented. One 2015 estimate concluded that on Snapchat, a photo-sharing platform that is especially popular with children and teens, users share 8,796 images every second and well over 30 million images per hour.[47] However, the most profound shift to occur with the rise of digital media, and specifically social media, may be the potential audience that now exists for one's private images.

For many decades, photographs and other media, including home movies, existed only in single copies or as limited editions. A photograph of a special occasion might have been printed out in doubles or triples, and a home video of an event such as a wedding might have been duplicated for close friends and relatives, but in most instances photographs and home movies rarely traveled far beyond the private sphere of the home. As we near the end of the second decade of the twenty-first century, the context of private photographs has greatly expanded. If early photographs were carefully staged but rarely cir-culated, we now live in an era when little thought at all goes into the composition of photographs, yet their potential circulation has grown unfathomably wide. The same holds true for moving images. If shooting a home movie was once an elaborate and costly endeavor that entailed careful planning and selection, in the twenty-first century, it has become just one of a number of daily screen-based activities, from streaming videos to FaceTiming with friends. At no cost and in virtually no time, representations of the most quotidian moments can now be broadcast to millions of viewers.

Once relegated to the margins, children and teens are no longer absent from images or represented merely through the eyes of adults, and this appears to hold true, albeit with some notable discrepancies, around the world.[48] As we near the end of the second decade of the twenty-first century, young people have access to both still and moving-image technologies and to the platforms needed to disseminate images. In the future, childhood and adolescence will increasingly be seen and understood through the lens of children and teens rather than that of adults. This is a welcome shift. If the destiny of a child of the 1950s or the 1970s was to end up as an actor in a silent family film orchestrated by the head of their household, children and teens are now empowered to direct, shoot, and star in their own movies. There is also a growing audience for young people's media creations. While most children and adolescents continue to produce media for friends and family, they can also reach a much wider audience.[49] The value of putting media into the hands of young people is not at issue here. The issue this book seeks to explore is what happens when these largely spontaneous representations of childhood and adolescence are not only widely and indefinitely circulated but also turned into data. After all, who is this "data subject," and how do they manage both to forget and to achieve the sometimes necessary and liberating experience of being forgotten?

2 Forgetting and Being Forgotten in the Age of the Data Subject

For children and adolescents, forgetting and being forgotten hold specific import. After all, the process of growing up is contingent on both forgetting one's younger self and having it forgotten by others—at least the parts of that self that one can't bear to carry forward into adulthood. As I contend in this book, digital media technologies interfere with this process. While the consequences of this interference are not yet fully known or understood, I am certainly not the only one concerned about the potential impact.

Recent attempts to enact legislation in support of the "right to be forgotten" have been driven at least in part by concerns about children and youth. A proposal by the European Commission (EC) on the right to be forgotten originally paid particular attention to young "data subjects": "The data subject shall have the right to obtain from the controller the erasure of personal data relating to them and the abstention of further dissemination of such data, especially in relation to personal data made available by the data subject while he or she was a child."[1] In a 2012 speech, Viviane Reding, then vice president of the EC, underscored this point: "It is the individual who should be in the best position to protect the privacy of their data by choosing whether or not to provide it. It is therefore important to empower EU citizens, particularly teenagers, to be in control of their own identity online."[2] When the European Union's General Data Protection Regulation finally came into effect in 2018, the legislation still contained provisions concerning the collection and processing of data belonging to children under the age of sixteen.[3]

Young data subjects have also been singled out for protection in other jurisdictions. Since 2015, California minors, but not adults, have had the right to request that information they post online be removed, and the state's businesses must notify all minors and their parents of this right.[4] The California legislation, however, applies only to material a young person has posted online themselves, not to material posted by others. Emerging legislation in the United Kingdom goes much further. In preparation for the country's exit from the European Union, UK legislators have been working to draft data erasure laws that would replace and extend the reach of the European General Data Protection Regulation. The United Kingdom's Data Protection Bill, drafted in September 2017, contains twenty-three mentions of the word "child" and provides strong protection for children and teens.[5]

That data erasure laws in both Europe and North America have focused on young people is not entirely surprising, since these laws reflect the common assumption that children and adolescents lack sound judgment. But minors' ability to judge what to post online is not my focus here. Rather, I explore the importance of the right to be forgotten—and the right to forget, which is frequently contingent on being forgotten by others—particularly for young people. Growing up is as much a process of forgetting and being forgotten as it is an accumulation of knowledge and experiences. As a result, long-standing concerns about children, adolescents, and the media need to be radically rethought. Instead of asking how to protect young people from online predators, the real question we should be asking is how to protect them from themselves and, more specifically, from the selves they may eventually wish to leave behind as they arrive in adulthood.

Reparative Perspectives on Forgetting

Collective forgetting, like collective memory, is generally understood as a social phenomenon. While there are certainly many reasons why people forget en masse, collective forgetting is nearly always characterized in negative terms. This is not surprising, since it often involves a form of forgetting that supports a specific political mandate, such as forgetting about the legacy of colonialism or slavery.[6] By contrast, individual forgetting is often represented as a reparative process by philosophers, psychoanalysts, and experimental psychologists.

In *On the Genealogy of Morality,* Friedrich Nietzsche concludes that forgetting might simply be a matter of shutting the doors and windows of consciousness. Just as one might close the door of one's study to focus on work, from time to time one needs to close off one's consciousness:

> To shut the doors and windows of consciousness for a while; not to be bothered by the noise and battle with which our underworld of serviceable organs work with and against each

other; a little peace, a little *tabula rasa* of consciousness to make room for something new, above all for the nobler functions and functionaries, for ruling, predicting, pre-determining (our organism runs along oligarchic lines, you see)—that, as I said, is the benefit of active forgetfulness, like a doorkeeper or guardian of mental order, rest and etiquette: from which we can immediately see how there could be no happiness, cheerfulness, hope, pride, *immediacy,* without forgetfulness.

Nietzsche is emphatic: for the person who cannot forget, there can be no happiness, no hope, and no immediacy. The person who cannot forget "cannot 'cope' with anything." And yet, he goes on to point to a strange and inherent contradiction in humans: "Precisely this necessarily forgetful animal, in whom forgetting is a strength, representing a form of *robust* health, has bred for himself a counter-device, memory, with the help of which forgetfulness can be suspended in certain cases." Rather than view forgetting as something that threatens memory, Nietzsche implores his readers to consider an opposite scenario—one in which memory threatens the necessary and welcome practice of forgetting. "Forgetfulness is not just a *vis inertiae,* as superficial people believe," he insists, "but is rather an active ability to suppress, positive in the strongest sense of the word."[7]

Since Nietzsche, other reparative readings of forgetting have been put forward by thinkers across disciplines. Sigmund Freud's observation that we frequently forget or distort events as a way to cope with those things we find intolerable or traumatic is likely the most well known reparative reading of forgetting, but it is certainly not the only attempt to substantiate forgetting's potential function. In his 1932 work *Remembering,* the psychologist Frederic

Bartlett remarked that forgetting may hold "great psychological importance."[8] More recently, a growing body of work has emphasized the benefits of forgetting. The neuroscientists Michael Anderson and Simon Hanslmayr have further developed the concept of "motivated forgetting." Like Nietzsche, who suggests that forgetting is necessary to maintain some semblance of happiness, cheerfulness, hope, and pride, Anderson and Hanslmayr argue that "to sustain positive emotions or concentration, belief in some state of affairs, confidence, or optimism, it may be necessary to reduce accessibility of experiences that undermine those states."[9] Likewise, the experimental psychologist Benjamin Storm observes, "As frustrating as forgetting might seem, we are far better with it than we would be without it."[10] In the era of digital media, however, the once taken-for-granted ability to "shut the doors and windows of consciousness for a while" is now at risk.

In the twenty-first century, even Nietzsche's metaphor takes on a profoundly different meaning. The word "window," after all, is now more likely to conjure up the window on a screen than the architectural feature to which he originally alluded. But closing the windows on our devices is profoundly different from closing the windows in our home. Closing the windows and drawing the curtains prevents us from seeing out, but it also prevents the world from peering in. When we close the windows on a digital device we can no longer see out (what's online is closed off), but this act does not prevent others from peering in. While we take a rest, others can and do continue to monitor us (even taking note of our inactivity). The window metaphor aptly underscores the difference between the experience of forgetting and being forgotten in an analogue and a digital world.

If the experiences of forgetting and being forgotten were once intertwined, this is no longer the case. In the digital world, we can close our windows or even go entirely off the grid. But when we log off, even though we reduce our digital footprint (the data we leave behind), our data shadows (the information others generate about us) continue to multiply. In short, the individual's desire to forget (to shut their windows, delete their data, go off line, and disconnect) has little bearing on being forgotten by others, because the data subject remains active even as the living individual to which it is linked lies dormant. Our data subject continues to expand and gain notoriety without our knowledge, troubling attempts to achieve the "active forgetting" that Nietzsche deemed so necessary for mental health and contentment. It is on this basis that the legal scholar Antoinette Rouvroy suggests that what we may be witnessing now is a radical reversal of Nietzsche's formula:

> All this suggests, in particular, the possibility of an inversion of the relationship between memory and oblivion: the "capacity of forgetting," *biologically inscribed in the human being,* a condition of a robust health according to Nietzsche, giving way to a non-biological "faculty of memory." . . . While humanity has historically struggled against the limits of memory, with forgetfulness prevailing by default, we now seem to be engaged in a process whereby the relationship between forgetfulness and memory is being reversed. By default, all information (sound, visual, textual) will soon be recorded and kept in a digital form, and forgetting, which requires the active erasure of data, will become the exception rather than the rule.[11]

But what are the consequences of active forgetting no longer being able to override the pervasive memory of data, especially for children and adolescents?

Subjects without Boundaries and Curfews

At the center of discussions on the right to be forgotten is a new and still ambiguous social actor—the "data subject." Despite the widespread use of the term in legal literature, defining who or what a data subject is remains challenging. In some contexts, the data subject refers to a set of data relating to a particular subject. In other cases, the term is used to describe any identified or identifiable "natural person." But the concept usually points neither exclusively to a set of data nor to a natural person, but rather to a relationship between the two. The data subject is, in this respect, defined by his or her (or its) relationship to a natural person. For example, my data subject exists to the extent that I also exist, but this is where things begin to unravel. After all, when I die (i.e., when I am no longer a material presence in this world), my data subject may persist. While the data subject is initially dependent on the existence of a natural person, it may over time accrue enough agency to "outlive" the person to which it was once tethered. This explains why some people now have "social media wills."[12] This is also precisely why child and teen data subjects merit special consideration.

Although people of all ages change over time, children and teens are especially subject to change. One is generally a very different person at nine than at thirteen, and then again at twenty-two. The problem that faces young data subjects is that one's nine-year-old and thirteen-year-old data subjects may outlive their welcome and interfere with the ability to get on with one's emerging adult life. While earlier generations of young adults may also have faced the occasional return of their young selves (e.g., in the form of an embarrassing family photograph or high school yearbook), these selves

(or representations of selves) had strict boundaries and curfews—
they were not nearly as free to roam across space and time.

To date, the most fully realized response to the indiscriminate and
seemingly effortless remembering of data subjects is the concept of
the right to be forgotten. This right, which now informs data erasure
legislation in Europe and continues to gain interest from legal
scholars in other jurisdictions around the world, recognizes that in
the digital world, where remembering has become so pervasive, we
occasionally need to intervene to correct the balance.[13] The Dutch
legal theorist Bert-Jaap Koops proposes that three interrelated
assumptions with broader legal, ethical, and social implications
underpin the right to be forgotten. First, one might see the legislation as promoting a "clean slate" or "fresh start." This concept already informs several areas of law, including juvenile criminal law
and credit reporting, and is designed to promote a healthy form of
"social forgetting." But Koops identifies two additional assumptions:
"A social perspective that outdated negative information should
not be used against people," and "an individual self-development
perspective that people should feel unrestrained in expressing themselves in the here and now, without fear of future consequences." For
Koops, at stake in the right to be forgotten is not only the right to avoid
having one's past dragged indiscriminately back into the present, but
also the right to not be confronted with one's past in a way that would
disrupt one's ability to forget. Koops notes that the right to be forgotten "highlights the importance of being able to forget and of being
able to act without fear that your current actions may haunt you for
the rest of your life."[14]

It seems reasonable to conclude that forgetting is important for
many reasons, including individual self-development. Where there
is no forgetting, or where forgetting is the exception rather than the

rule, minor risk-taking activities, including those that are part and parcel of growing up, will become too risky to carry out. If adolescents were once more or less free to shapeshift their style, trying on different outfits, politics, and identities, there is now a risk that these "phases" (as they are often disparagingly labeled by adults) will be permanently enshrined online and will define the individual well beyond the moment in which they were adopted. But at what cost? Whether one exposes too much and pays the price, or is overly cautious and avoids taking the sorts of risks that are part of self-discovery, living in a world where forgetting and being forgotten are increasingly out of reach has consequences.

Forgetting and Identity Development in the Digital Age

Today, even minor incidents are endlessly repeated in the echo chamber of the internet. Somewhat surprisingly, however, this was not always the case. Early on, the internet promised to provide an exceptionally safe space for exploring the extremes of one's politics, identity, and desires without consequence.[15]

In the 1990s, the ability to leave the material world behind—and along with it, all its worries and shameful moments—was widely extolled as the internet's greatest promise. It was this promise that informed my earliest research on online communities and youth. In early 1997, which was even before the term "blog" had been coined, I started to research the personal websites of transgender-identified youth. Roaming from one community to the next in the web-hosting site GeoCities, I discovered dozens of young people using the web as a way to inhabit a gender identity that did not match their assigned gender at birth. Transgender rights had not yet become a topic of widespread public debate, and there was very little public awareness on the specific needs of transgender youth. What I discovered in these early online spaces—most of them located in GeoCities' "West-Hollywood" community, where, as in the real West Hollywood, everyone was welcome to express their sexuality and gender as they pleased—were virtual spaces where otherwise vulnerable youth were able to freely explore their identities at low risk. This lack of risk was largely due to the way people chose to use the web at this time and due to the web's technical limitations. There were no photographs or videos on these early websites; most of them contained only texts and clip art. The creators rarely attached their own names or locations to their sites and had no real reason to do so. For the transgender youth in my study, the internet presented itself as a safe place to try on an aspect of their identities they could not explore in their material lives.[16]

In the 1990s, a surprisingly high number of people turned to the internet precisely because it promised to liberate them from the shackles of the material world and from their own histories. It was, in a sense, embraced because it was seen as a space of forgetting. As the sociologist Sherry Turkle wrote in her 1995 book *Life on the Screen,* "When we step through the screen into virtual communities, we reconstruct our identities on the other side of the looking glass."[17] This process, Turkle contended at the time, offered us unlimited access to explore and role-play new identities. But she remained cautious, warning, "We are dwellers on the threshold between the real and virtual, unsure of our footing, inventing ourselves as we go along."[18] Yet, by and large, Turkle's early work on online communities was consistent with a broader belief at the time that the internet held the potential to set us free.[19]

In *Life on the Screen,* Turkle focused on online gaming worlds and multiuser domains (MUDs), which permitted anyone with a computer, internet connection, and basic computer skills to reinvent themselves however they liked and explore the alternate universes then proliferating online. In these spaces, noted Turkle, "The characters need not be human and there are more than two genders. Players are invited to help build the computer world itself. Using a relatively simple programming language, they can create a room in the game space where they are able to set the stage and define the rules." These worlds were open to people of all ages. In one space, Turkle reported encountering an eleven-year-old player who built a room she called "the condo": "It is beautifully furnished. She has created magical jewelry and makeup for her dressing table. When she visits the condo, she invites her cyber friends to join her there, she chats, orders virtual pizza, and flirts."[20]

For children and teens growing up in the 1990s (and even for many adults at the time), this was precisely the internet's appeal. Cut off from the "real world" and more closely linked to the geek culture of games such as Dungeons and Dragons than to reality, the internet was a place for fantasy, role-playing, and identity experiments. While it is true that at least some people spent those early years of the internet engaged in far more mundane tasks (e.g., setting up a Hotmail account or learning how to carry out online research), for many others it was a place to abandon one's material life, biology, and assumed identity—to leave one's gender, race, age, and physical constraints behind and live out other identities in other worlds. It was a place to get away from it all—to adopt a new name, play out kinky sexual fantasies, and enter MUDs to switch genders and even species. This feature, Turkle contended, made the internet a critical space of identity development, especially for youth.[21]

To support her point, Turkle turned to the work of the psychoanalyst Erik Erikson, specifically to his concept of a psychosocial "moratorium." In *Childhood and Society,* published in 1950, Erikson argued that the adolescent mind "is essentially a mind of the *moratorium,* a psychosocial stage between childhood and adulthood, and between the morality learned by the child, and the ethics to be developed by the adult."[22] Despite his choice of words, Erikson did not consider adolescence to be a period of delayed experience. The moratorium, explained Turkle, "is not on significant experiences but on their consequences."[23] Both Turkle and Erikson, while recognizing that all experiences have consequences, contended that adolescence is generally understood to be a time of risk-free experimentation, and that this experimentation serves a specific societal purpose.[24] In his 1968 book *Identity: Youth in Crisis,* Erikson described the psychosocial moratorium as "a period that is characterized by a selective permissiveness on the part of society and a provocative playfulness on the part of youth." "Each society and each culture," he continued, "institutionalizes a certain moratorium for the majority of its young people.... The moratorium may be a time for horse stealing and vision-quests, a time for *Wanderschaft* or work 'out West' or 'down under,' a time for 'lost youth' or academic life, a time for self-sacrifice or for pranks."[25] Whether one is on a vision quest or working at a ski resort or just skipping class to party, this moratorium has long served a very important purpose. In Turkle's words, "the moratorium facilitates the development of a core self, a personal sense of what gives life meaning."[26]

Of course, Erikson and Turkle were writing in different eras. In the early 1950s, when *Childhood and Society* was first published, and even in the early 1960s, when the revised edition was issued, Erikson was living in and reflecting on a world where it was easier to view adolescence and even college years as a sort of "time out" where a young person was free to experiment with relatively few consequences—that is, if they had the gender and race privilege to do so. By the time

Turkle was writing *Life on the Screen,* in the early 1990s, the world was in flux. College-age students were facing an increasingly competitive job market and a sluggish economy, and the AIDS crisis had changed the stakes of sexual experimentation—suddenly, the worst consequence of having sex was not heartbreak or unplanned pregnancy but death. But this is precisely why Turkle believed online communities were coming to play such a critical role in the lives of adolescents. Virtual communities, she insisted, "offer permission to play, to try things out. This is part of what makes them attractive."[27] If the adolescent "moratorium" is understood as a critical stage of personal development—a period of experimentation when one can try out various rituals, creeds, and programs as part of a larger process of "searching for social values which guide identity"—the internet promised a space where such reckless experimentation could safely persist, even in a period of economic uncertainty and AIDS.[28]

In the end, however, the internet's development would take a radically different turn—one that is now compromising the very concept of an adolescent moratorium on consequences. The moratorium is based on a shared societal understanding that adolescence is a time when young people should be able to take certain risks in the name of "finding themselves" and even make a few mistakes along the way. But in the second decade of the twenty-first century, the spaces where such self-discovery can safely be carried out without consequence are rapidly shrinking.

By the early 2000s, the web was already becoming a radically different space. With the arrival of social media platforms, beginning with Facebook in 2004, people's online posts became increasingly tethered to their natural self. While it may not have been obvious at the time, from the outset, social media platforms were about closing the gap between the virtual and the real, a gap that had originally been a defining feature of the internet. Fantasy spaces continued to flourish (e.g., in the virtual world Second Life), and they still persist in online gaming, but social media would ultimately prove far more popular and pervasive than the web's early fantasy-driven spaces ever were. As reality came to dominate online spaces, however, another shift took place: online spaces began to require users to register using their real-life identities. The days of creating email accounts without any verification of one's actual identity were already long gone. A growing number of sites were also becoming linked to pay-per-view or pay-for-use services. For adolescents, a large amount of material was now behind pay gates and was accessible only with a parent's permission and credit card. At the same time, for adults, more mundane aspects of daily life, such as banking and managing utility bills, started to move online. As a result, teens could no longer count on even the most Luddite parents being ignorant of the online world. Once a mysterious portal to another world where one could adopt an alternative gender, don wings, or have sex with mythical creatures, the web started to look a lot more like everyday life. Unbeknownst to many users at the time, this is also when our digital footprints started to accumulate at a much more rapid pace. By the end of the first decade of the new millennium, the realm once known as "cyberspace" (a concept appropriately borrowed from the pages of science fiction), which had promised to help us forget who we really were, had become, instead, an obstacle to forgetting and being forgotten.

Reestablishing a Psychosocial Moratorium

As recruiters and human resources specialists readily admit, few hires are now made without at least a preliminary online search. Many recruiters even hire third parties to dig up data on job candidates that may not be easily retrievable with an initial Google search. Candidates are also frequently rejected on the basis of the unflattering impression left by their digital footprint.[29] But job recruiters are not the only people taking notice. Prospective spouses are now also subject to extensive online searches, often by extended family members, and so too are applicants for everything from coworking spaces to summer camps. Where an interview once sufficed, a search is increasingly the norm. Everyone, in a sense, has become the sum of their online archives.[30] But with this shift, something profoundly important is lost—the psychosocial moratorium that at least some youth in some contexts once took for granted. The question then becomes, How can we restore this moratorium, and even expand it?

Data erasure legislation is one response, especially legislation directed at minors (such as Privacy Rights for California Minors in the Digital World). Yet, such piecemeal laws on their own are probably inadequate for re-establishing a psychosocial moratorium for youth. Young people around the world are already deeply implicated in digital life as both consumers and producers. Granting special data erasure rights to some youth in some jurisdictions would not solve the broader problem.

What if instead of legal grounds, the moratorium were established on technical grounds? In *Delete: The Virtue of Forgetting in the Digital Age,* Viktor Mayer-Schönberger argues that it is time to "reset" the balance and "make forgetting just a tiny bit easier again than remembering." His proposal does not call for any sweeping legal solutions; it hinges instead on several alternatives, including a technical solution that seeks to mimic human forgetting by allowing users to set expiration dates for information stored online. Such expiration dates, he explains, "are not about imposed forgetting.

They are about awareness and human action, and about asking humans to reflect—if only for a few moments—how long the information they want to store may remain valuable and useful."[31] At first glance, the proposal sounds both reasonable and viable, but would such a solution be widely embraced? That is, is there really a collective desire for digital information to disappear over time, especially among children and adolescents? On this account, Snapchat stands as a particularly compelling example.

Snapchat was launched in 2011 as a social media platform that enabled texts and images to be shared for only a limited amount of time. After being viewed, "snaps" would be automatically deleted. Targeted primarily to millennials but quickly embraced by a younger demographic, including many children, the platform at first appeared to offer just the sort of moratorium that would enable young people to share and connect with others online without long-term consequences. In theory, with Snapchat, a person could share a silly or even compromising text or image without any fear that it would come back to haunt them. (In fact, the photographs are cached after being removed from the server, but they are rendered difficult to retrieve since the file extension is changed.) Early on, Snapchat was seen as a welcome addition to the social media market, and it was even embraced by some parents of younger social media users as a "safer" option than Instagram or Facebook. This support quickly dissolved, however, when critics began to regard the app's built-in capacity to delete images as a feature that was promoting risk-taking behaviors, especially among young users. It didn't take long for the app to come under attack as a device engineered for sexting. The social media scholar danah boyd contends that this perception was largely promoted by journalists.[32]

In reality, neither the app's claims to ephemerality nor its critics' claims that it was used primarily for sexting proved to be entirely true. The original version of Snapchat did limit users' ability to store images and texts, though it was not the case that the images simply disappeared after being shared. Savvy users quickly learned how to get around these limitations; they would take screenshots of images shared on the app and then preserve or recirculate them on other platforms.[33] Several studies on how and why people were using Snapchat also revealed that the sexting rumors were exaggerated. In a 2014 survey of over a hundred adults, only 1.6 percent of respondents reported using Snapchat primarily for sexting; 14.2 percent reported having occasionally used it for this purpose; and almost a quarter, 23.6 percent, reported using it for what the survey categorized as "joke sexting"—sending sexual or pseudo-sexual content as a joke.[34] In her work on teens and social media, boyd reached a similar conclusion: "Asking teens about Snapchat," she writes, "I found most were using the app to signal that an image wasn't meant for posterity. They shared inside jokes, silly pictures, and images that were funny only in the moment. Rather than viewing photographs as an archival production, they saw the creation and sharing of these digital images as akin to an ephemeral gesture. And they used Snapchat to signal this expectation."[35]

Snapchat merits specific attention here because of its unique relationship to time and memory. On the one hand, users seem to enjoy Snapchat because of its promise of ephemerality. On the other hand, they have been quick to subvert the platform's ephemeral nature. It was snappers, not Snapchat, who were initially responsible for finding creative ways to capture and store snaps. Eventually the company followed their lead, introducing a timer setting appropriately called "infinity," which allows permanent access to snaps.[36] What the Snapchat example underscores is that young people would likely reject any intervention designed to place expiration dates on the information they generate and post online.

While the reasons for this rejection are no doubt complex, one factor may be that sentimentality and nostalgia run especially high among tweens and teens and often manifest themselves in collections of all kinds. Anyone who has recently been a tween or teen (or currently lives with one) will appreciate that adolescents frequently insist on keeping even the most superfluous items (ticket stubs, playbills, ski-lift passes, bottle caps, outgrown T-shirts, and so on). These objects are not exactly souvenirs but rather, in the words of the literary critic Susan Stewart, "kitsch objects"—consumer objects whose value is not monetary but rather inscribed with some sort of collective practice or experience or identity. They are, Stewart suggests, "souvenirs of an era not of a self," and this is also why they "tend to accumulate around a period of intense socialization, adolescence."[37] These objects enable adolescents to believe in the illusion that they can hold on to the very things they can't bear to let go (e.g., an intense relationship or especially memorable experience). In the digital age adolescents are still collecting, but in addition to material photographs (e.g., strips of photographs snapped in photo booths) and physical artifacts, they are now also accumulating digital artifacts. The Snapchat example suggests that any attempt to place expiration dates on data—even those set by individual users—may face a powerful opponent: adolescents' often strong feelings of attachment to artifacts of all kinds, including digital ones. While adolescents' sentimentality and nostalgia may pose an unexpected challenge to forgetting, however, twenty-first-century forgetting faces far greater obstacles.

3　Screens, Screen Memories, and Childhood Celebrity

P redicting the long-term impact of growing up with one's childhood and youth forever present is difficult in part because it is an experience with few historical analogues. One notable exception is the fate of childhood celebrities. This topic is so frequently mined in television exposés and entertainment magazines that anyone could probably recount at least one story about a young celebrity's demise. If these stories are the stock-in-trade of tabloids, it is likely because they nearly always follow a predictable narrative arc and focus on a single character who requires no introduction. Embedded in these typically sordid tales is also a common assumption: overexposure as a youth is dangerous—a nearly certain pathway to substance abuse, crime, imprisonment, or even early death. Sadly, there appears to be at least some truth to this assumption.

One of the most frequently repeated cautionary tales about the dangers of childhood celebrity is that of the three young actors who played a set of siblings in the 1970s sitcom *Diff'rent Strokes*. In the sitcom, a widower named Mr. Drummond adopts two African American brothers—Arnold and Wilson Jackson—after their mother (his maid) dies. The boys move from Harlem to the Upper East Side to live with Drummond and his teenage daughter, Kimberly, in their sprawling Park Avenue apartment. The sitcom balanced humor with more serious topics ranging from racism and drug abuse to child abduction and rape. In the decades following the program's cancellation, all three of *Diff'rent Strokes'* child actors continued to make headlines, but not as actors. First, Gary Coleman, who played Arnold, sued his parents and manager for misappropriation of funds. Despite a million-dollar settlement, Coleman later filed for bankruptcy and ended up working as a security guard at a shopping mall. Following several highly publicized violent episodes, Coleman died of a brain injury at the age of forty-two.[1] By this time, his costar Dana Plato, who played Kimberly, had already committed suicide. Plato, like Coleman, struggled financially in the years following *Diff'rent Strokes*. Before her death at thirty-four, she held a series of minimum wage jobs, posed for *Playboy,* shot a soft porn movie (called *Different Strokes*), and held up a video store with a toy gun.[2] The only surviving child actor from the series is Todd Bridges, who played Willis. Although Bridges eventually returned to acting, he developed an addiction to cocaine that would ultimately result in his arrest. In an attempt to finally move beyond his past, in 2010, Bridges published a tell-all memoir, appropriately titled *Killing Willis*.[3] The problem facing Bridges, like many child celebrities, was that "killing" the person he was as an adolescent was unusually difficult because of the continued presence of his past identity (or at least of the fictional teen he once portrayed).

Despite the tabloid preoccupation with the fate of child actors, it would be misleading to suggest that all of them eventually go astray. For every Coleman, Plato, or Bridges, there is a child celebrity who moves on to a successful adult acting career or simply switches career tracks and lives a less visible life pursuing an unrelated line of work. The difference between child celebrities who thrive as adults and those who do not undoubtedly rests on myriad factors, but increasingly stringent regulations for child performers may be at least partially responsible for mitigating some of the long-term struggles that have historically plagued them. While not applicable in all jurisdictions, in U.S. film industry centers, including New York State and California, minors working in the theater or as television or film actors are protected by a wide range of labor and child protection laws. There are regulations stipulating when and for how long young performers can work, as well as ensuring that they can continue to attend school (or complete their high school diploma online or with the support of an on-set tutor). In both states, 15 percent of young performers' earnings must be transferred to a trust fund to ensure that they have at least some savings for the future. Other regulations aim to protect the health, morals, and general welfare of child performers.[4]

Still, not all child celebrities, even in New York and California, are currently covered by these protective regulations. With the spread of social media, there are now a growing number of young celebrities whose finances, as well as health and well-being, fall outside labor laws and regulations designed to protect young entertainers.[5] To date, however, the short- and long-term impacts of this new form of child celebrity have received surprisingly little attention from psychologists, legal scholars, and media theorists. This may reflect the fact that social media celebrities do not have much in common with earlier generations of celebrities. Many of them have gained their stardom unintentionally, often as a result of private rather than public activities. Indeed, social media celebrities, including those who are babies, children, and teens, frequently are best known for letting people into their private and intimate worlds, including quotidian spaces from the bedroom to the kitchen table. In this respect, today's youngest social media celebrities may have more in common with the Dionne quintuplets than they do with most young actors. Five sisters born in Ontario in 1934, the Dionne quintuplets spent much of their childhood behind a glass wall at a government-operated amusement park known as Quintland. Like many of today's young social media celebrities, they were viewed by onlookers (an estimated 3 million over the course of a decade) in situ, through a one-way screen, as they engaged in activities such as playing and eating. Decades later, the surviving Dionne sisters were compensated by the provincial government for the abuse they suffered while on display as children.[6] But what will be the fate of today's child social media celebrities? As the following accounts show, this is a difficult question to answer in part because these celebrities are by no means a homogenous group. How they acquire their online fame entails varying degrees of awareness, agency, and complicity. The short- and long-term consequences for babies, children, and teens of online stardom may be as empowering as they are devastating.

Baby Pictures and Baby Memes

"Babies" is among the most popular categories of images on the internet. In many ways, the online obsession with babies is merely an extension of photography's longstanding preoccupation with them. Babies and children have been a popular subject since photography's invention, and camera manufacturers often used them to market new technologies. But with the emergence of digital photography and social media platforms, the number of baby photographs in circulation has drastically increased. So too have the types and uses of these photographs. It is difficult to know for certain how many photographs of babies and children are posted online every day, but at least one study suggests that the practice of posting pictures of one's children online is nearly universal. A 2016 study of 127 mothers found that 98 percent of them had uploaded a picture of their newborn to Facebook, and 80 percent of those mothers had featured the child on their profile picture.[7] In a 2015 survey of two thousand British parents, each parent posted, on average, nearly two hundred photographs of their child online each year, which means that most of the children had close to a thousand photographs in circulation online by the time they entered kindergarten at the age of five.[8]

In addition to an increase in the quantity of baby and child photographs and videos—which have become easier and less expensive to take and distribute since the arrival of digital photography, camera phones, and social media platforms—the content of these images has also changed. A 2015 poll of several hundred Americans revealed that most parents now use social media (84 percent of mothers and 70 percent of fathers). Among these parents, a majority (74 percent) knew of at least one parent who they believed had "overshared" about their child online, and 56 percent reported having encountered embarrassing information about a child posted by another parent. In addition, 51 percent reported that other parents had exposed their child's whereabouts on a social media platform, and 27 percent reported parents posting inappropriate photographs of their child.[9] While it is certainly the case that some parents have always had bad judgment—for example, choosing to shoot a home movie of their two-year-old's potty training trials and then projecting it at the child's thirteenth-birthday party—in the past, such incidents were relatively uncommon. A parent would have had to possess a strong desire to film an event like this to go through the effort of loading film into a camera just in time to capture it. Since such images had to be developed by a third party, there was also the possibility that they would later be censored by a vigilant developer at a processing plant. Today, by contrast, parents frequently already have a phone equipped with a camera in their hand or pocket while they are engaged in everyday household and childrearing tasks. Combined with the fact that one can now circulate images without the intervention of a third party, spontaneous and often inappropriate images of babies and children continue to proliferate online. But what and why are parents sharing and, in many cases, oversharing?

At least one study found that the phenomenon of circulating photos and accounts of children, often known as "sharenting," is more common among mothers, especially new mothers, than fathers.[10] Some researchers speculate that this is because mothers are typically more likely to end up at home alone caring for young children, and social media sharing is one way to break the isolation. But this is not to suggest that fathers do not share and overshare as well. As I was writing this chapter, the father and blogger Jesse Mab-Phea Hill posted on Facebook a written account and several photographs about a stinky incident in his home. Hill was about to enjoy a relaxing afternoon of cake eating and YouTube video watching when he detected a foul smell. After ruling out a mishap by one of his dogs, he went upstairs to check on his toddler. What he saw next was worse than expected: "There she is, standing at the baby gate, butt naked, holding her diaper, covered head to toe in her own crap. Im not talking a little poop here and there on her. I'm talking layered on globs of human fecal matter covering her arms, legs, face and HAIR."[11] In his brief absence, his toddler had spread fecal matter not only all over herself but all over her room. He included photographs of both his daughter and the filthy mess she left in her bedroom. Hill's account struck a chord with a surprising number of people. Within days, his post had been shared over a hundred thousand times, and magazines and newspapers around the world (ironically, including *Good Housekeeping*) had published reports on Hill's fecal fiasco. To be clear, there are no signs from the post or photographs that Hill wished any harm on his daughter, and in fact, the vast majority of the people who left comments in response to the post welcomed his humorous confession about this unglamorous aspect of parenting. But what about his daughter? How will she feel when she eventually discovers (or her friends or classmates discover) that her first widely recognized moment in life was as a feces-covered toddler?

For most parents, posting images of their children online is simply a way to share the joys—and the trials and tribulations—of parenting with family and friends and, in some cases, with a larger virtual community. But for a few parents, the impulse to share is driven by other factors, including monetary ones.

There are now a growing number of young celebrities whose treatment and earnings are not protected by any regulations. They include kids like Gavin, whose moods and facial expressions earned him celebrity status in the online world of memes. From 2013, when Gavin first entered his meme life at the age of two, up to the present, Gavin has had little control over his celebrity. His thirty-year-old uncle, Nick Mastodon, who was previously well known for his provocative postings on Vine (a video sharing app), was the original mastermind behind Gavin's rise to fame.[12] As the memes proliferated,

Gavin's mother, Katie Thomas, also started to circulate them. It didn't take long for Gavin to become one of the most widely circulated of child memes, but it is not clear whether he has ever been fully aware of his celebrity or in control of its benefits. Gavin's uncle and mother have both publicly stated that an effort is being made to put money aside for Gavin's "college fund," but how much revenue Gavin has already generated directly and indirectly through his meme "work" (in addition to his social media appearances, his mother sells T-shirts featuring his image for $20 each) and how much money is being saved is unknown.[13] What is clear is that unlike a child actor working on stage or on set—at least in jurisdictions with strict child entertainer laws—there are no regulations specifying who can benefit from Gavin's earnings; nor is there any way to put limits on how his everyday life has been and likely will continue to be exposed and disrupted in the future.

But Gavin is only one of numerous children in this situation. Since 2010, a growing number of parents, guardians, grandparents, and other relatives and friends have started to put videos and photographs of babies and children into circulation online. While most of these posts are meant for family and friends, others are intended to get attention or procure a modest financial gain. This is presumably the case for Matthew. Matthew's dad, Mike Chau, a New Yorker and foodie, has posted over a thousand Yelp reviews since 2012. Before his son's birth he was already leaving extended reviews on the platform, but his posts following Matthew's arrival are the ones for which he finally gained attention. Chau's reviews are unlike most Yelp reviews—they always include a picture of baby Matthew. From Matthew's uninterested glances over plates of high-brow pasta to his enthusiastic approval for a piece of pistachio cake with chocolate sauce, Matthew has gained a solid following on Yelp. This means that his father is now regularly courted by New York restaurant owners, who offer free meals to the entire Chau family in an attempt to garner a positive review on Yelp.[14] But will Matthew eventually come to resent his father for exploiting his cute toddler antics in restaurants across New York City? And would he ever be able to take legal action for invasion of privacy?

While some baby social media celebrities, like Hill's daughter, might find it difficult to hold their parents accountable were they to take legal action in the future (Hill's intent appears to have been neither malicious nor driven by a desire for monetary gain), others might have a more substantial basis upon which to launch a case. After all, if Gavin had launched his career as a traditional child celebrity (e.g., working as a stage or film actor), depending on his location, both his conditions of labor and his earnings would have been regulated from the outset. Since his celebrity was launched by his uncle on the social media site Vine, however, this was not a possibility. Most baby memes begin to generate income in ways that would never involve a contract at all—typically, a parent or another relative generates income using click-based advertisements placed on a personal website or YouTube channel in which the child meme is featured. Setting the legal considerations aside, however, it is important to consider some of the other potential costs. One of these has to do with what we remember about our childhoods.

People generally remember more positive than negative memories. Indeed, some studies have found that adults remember twice as many positive as negative autobiographical events. Moreover, positive memories are more common in older than in younger adults. This is good news, since positive memories promote happiness, and people tend to thrive when they are experiencing positive rather than negative emotions (e.g., joy versus shame or depression). The psychologist

Simon Nørby suggests several explanations for the prevalence of positive memories: "One reason . . . seems to be that positive events are more frequent than negative events. . . . Another reason may be the existence of a reminiscence 'bump' with respect to positive, but not negative, memories from young adulthood." And a third possible reason, according to Nørby, is that "people seem to selectively forget negative experiences." He suggests that this kind of forgetting cannot be dismissed as a mere failure of memory. The selective forgetting of negative experiences, including those from young adulthood, would be helpful because, he proposes, "if otherwise healthy people were preoccupied with negative memories most of the time, they would feel miserable."[15] But if this is the case, what is at stake for all the babies and toddlers whose childhood experiences are being documented and put into circulation online in ways that will cause them to continue reappearing over time? While Jesse Hill and most of the more than one hundred thousand people who enjoyed his Facebook post on parenting may have had a positive experience reading his story and viewing the accompanying photographs, there is no guarantee that his daughter will reencounter the incident in such a positive light in another ten or twenty years. What is certain is that in the past, thanks largely to the tendency to forget potentially shameful childhood experiences, Hill's daughter likely would never have been forced to confront this memory at all.

Adolescent Social Media Celebrities

To be clear, not all young online celebrities are the product of an adult's intervention—many older children and teens are self-made celebrities who have cultivated a following entirely of their own accord. In 2015, *Rolling Stone* published an article about Christian

Akridge, otherwise known as Christian Leave. Before Christian rose to fame on the now defunct Vine app, he was much like any other fourteen-year-old boy. Partial to haphazardly assembled casual wear that looked like it had come directly off the sale rack at Old Navy, and always ready to share an excrement joke, Christian was bored, contemplating applying for a part-time job at a taco restaurant, and wasting a lot of time online. His comedic videos, however, struck a chord with people on Vine, and within months he had amassed a following of over one hundred thousand viewers. This soon landed Christian a coveted spot at a PressPlay event (a live touring event where fans can meet their favorite social media stars in person). While a teenager wearing khaki shorts and specializing in potty humor might not sound appealing, many young fans, especially adolescent girls, prefer social media sensations like Christian over traditional celebrities. With their constant postings on Twitter, YouTube, and other social media apps, these celebrities are able to create the illusion of having a "real relationship" with fans—one that many fans feel is more authentic than the relationships they have with famous musicians or actors. Unlike young Gavin or Matthew, Christian is clearly in control of his image, or nearly in control (his parents, he said, made him remove one video in which he holds hands with another boy because they did not want anyone to be misled about his sexuality). However, for the most part, Christian's rise to fame has been of his own making and, so far, has offered more rewards than drawbacks. While he did opt to be homeschooled (his social media stardom was causing him to miss too many days of school), since his PressPlay tour, Christian has been able to successfully monetize his social media celebrity.[16]

Christian is not alone. There are now enough adolescent social media stars to support PressPlay and several similar live touring events. While most of the celebrities on these tours are young men, and most of the fans are tween and teen girls, there are at least a few young women who, like their male counterparts, specialize in delivering teen-targeted humor to other teens.[17] Alli Fitzpatrick, who got her start on Vine and later became a YouTube celebrity, has several million followers. Fitzpatrick's rise to fame was entirely her own doing. Her mother, Margaret, did not even learn of Alli's fame until she attended an event in New York City with her daughter. When the mother encountered a horde of girls crying and chanting Alli's name, she was so surprised, she wondered, "Are they talking about my Alli?"[18] But this kind of surprise is not unusual. Parents of social media celebrities with hundreds of thousands or even over a million followers often do not discover their child's online fame until promoters and agents start calling their home.[19] But the young online "celebrities" who are most at risk are not personalities like Christian or Alli, who have carefully crafted a persona and have received considerable recognition from both fans and promoters. They are children and teens who have acquired celebrity without intention or consent.

The Rise of Cyberbullying

One of the earliest known examples of what is now known as cyberbullying can be traced to a series of videos featuring a boy called the Star Wars Kid.[20] The original video was made in 2002—two years before the launch of YouTube—by a fifteen-year-old high school student in Trois-Rivières, Québec. At the time, Ghyslain Raza had no intention of becoming an internet meme, which was still an emerging concept.[21] In fact, Raza was just having fun in his high school's film studio when he shot a video of himself wielding a makeshift light saber and clumsily imitating a character from the *Star Wars* series.

The videocassette, which he accidently left on a table at the school, was found by a classmate, and several months later, in early 2003, another classmate uploaded it to the internet. Raza did not post the video himself, nor did he ever intend for it to go viral. At the time, it likely did not even occur to Raza that it would be possible for his video to be viewed by hundreds of thousands of people. In the end, the video garnered substantial attention not only online but also offline, as traditional media sources began to report on the new phenomenon with which his video was becoming synonymous. In May 2003, for example, the *New York Times* reported, "Since it was released on the Web late last month as a prank by fellow high school students who discovered the clip, the video has been downloaded more than a million times. Also in circulation are several 'remixes,' adding special effects to make the stick glow like a light saber and setting the action to music." The article continued, "Short videos of embarrassing, funny or illicit moments are common Internet fare. But this one, known as the *Star Wars Kid,* has traveled farther, faster, and commanded more attention than any in recent memory."[22]

For Raza, the impact of accidentally becoming the world's first widely circulated internet meme was devastating. Immediately after the video began to circulate online, Raza lost the few friends he had and faced severe bullying at school. The bullying was so intense that Raza dropped out of school and ended up completing his school year from a children's psychiatric ward.[23] Not all reactions to the video were negative. Raza had gained fans, some of whom were moved enough to start an online fundraiser to purchase an iPod and Amazon gift certificate for him, but these gifts were of little consolation.

In July 2003, Raza's parents filed a lawsuit against the parents of the boys who had uploaded the video. The lawsuit was settled out of court. Even after Raza's parents took legal action, however, the video—by then far out of Raza's hands—continued to circulate. Today, it has had more than 27 million views on YouTube and has been parodied on everything from South Park to the Colbert Report.[24] The video, writes danah boyd, exemplifies "how mass public shaming is a byproduct of widespread internet attention and networked distribution."[25]

For many years, Raza distanced himself from the video and tried to reinvent his identity. In 2013, when he was a law student at McGill University, he finally came forward to talk about the episode with the hope of helping other kids deal with the rising problem of cyberbullying. In an interview with the French-language magazine L'actualité, he described the period of the video's release and aftermath as "very dark." "No matter how hard I tried to ignore people telling me to commit suicide," he explained, "I couldn't help but feel worthless, like my life wasn't worth living."[26] Ironically, by coming forward to speak out on the issue of cyberbullying, he also gave up any hope of ever moving beyond his status as the Star Wars Kid.

Since 2003, when Star Wars Kid was surreptitiously uploaded to the internet and became accessible to millions, the unintended circulation of photographs and videos online has become a growing problem, especially for adolescent girls, who are frequently victims of a specific type of cyberbullying. Since 2010, there have been dozens of reports about girls and young women taking their own lives after compromising photographs and videos of their bodies were circulated online.[27] Some of these cases involved young women sending sexual images to a boyfriend who later retaliated for a breakup by reposting the images. This phenomenon was initially described as "revenge porn" but is more accurately termed "intimate image abuse," "image-based abuse," or "nonconsensual sharing of intimate images." In other cases, which have now been documented around the world, the images were taken while the young woman was passed out, usually at a party, and was being sexually violated by one or more participants. For many girls, suicide has appeared to offer the only certain escape from the humiliation of the experience. This was certainly the case for Rehtaeh Parsons.[28]

Parsons had no intention of gaining online notoriety when she chose to attend a small house party with a few friends in 2011. At the party, Parsons, who was fifteen at the time and living in a suburb of Halifax, Nova Scotia, consumed hard liquor—enough to make her throw up—and at some point in the evening, she was assaulted by a group of teenage boys. Sadly, there is nothing unusual about this story so far—underage drinking and sexual assault are common among teens.[29] But in Parsons's case, what happened on the night of the party was just the beginning of a much longer ordeal. Within a few weeks, photographs of the party began to circulate online. In one photograph, she is nude from the waist down and a young man appears to be assaulting her. Tagged as a "slut" by her peers on various online platforms, Parsons soon found herself socially isolated and grappling with suicidal thoughts that neither a school transfer nor counseling could quell. To make matters worse, a police investigation concluded that there was insufficient evidence to press assault charges against the young men in the photograph. On April 4, 2013, less than two years after the incident, Parsons committed suicide. Following Parsons's death, two of the young men involved in the incident (then over the age of eighteen) were charged with the distribution of child pornography.[30] Parsons's story then took another disturbing turn.

In 2014, nearly three years after Parsons's death, a Canadian judge ruled that no one—neither journalists nor regular citizens—could state her name in newspapers, on television, over the radio, or on any social media platform. Although consistent with the Canadian

Criminal Code, which maintains that all trials involving child pornography are subject to a publication ban, this was a cruel turn of
events. By the time Parsons's case reached the courts, both of her
parents and many advocates had embraced her legacy as part of a
campaign to call for aggressive new laws on cyberbullying. To suddenly tell her parents, friends, and advocates that they were breaking
the law by even mentioning her name online felt like the revictim-
ization of a young woman whose death was the result of negative
online exposure. The following year, an independent report on the
handling of the case, commissioned by the province of Nova Scotia,
was published. The report's author, Murray D. Segal, noted how differently an episode like this would have played out before the introduction of the internet: "Years ago, adolescent mistakes could
quickly be forgotten. Today, that is no longer the case. Because the
consequences of adolescents' conduct are different, the rules must
be different."[31]

What the stories of Gavin, Matthew, Christian, Raza, and Parsons
reveal is that children and adolescents who become renowned online
cannot be easily grouped together. They range from babies and
toddlers who may have, at best, only a vague understanding of their
online celebrity, to self-made adolescent social media celebrities, to
victims of cyberbullying. They are a diverse group with different
needs and rights. We should take care that efforts to protect potential
victims of online exploitation or cyberbullying do not erode the rights
of those teens who decide to take their entertainment careers into
own hands. Indeed, the fact that young people can now not only represent themselves but also circulate these images is something to celebrate. Child and adolescent self-representation is not a problem, but
unregulated and continuous circulation of some of these photographs

and videos can be a problem under specific circumstances—namely, when the circulation compromises the psychosocial moratorium that has historically been granted to adolescents.

Here, it is useful to return briefly to Raza's case. Had Raza made his video and taken the cassette home in 2002, he likely would have watched it himself and possibly shared it with family and friends. Perhaps the video would have survived for a few more years, and he would have found it later—at eighteen or twenty years of age—and re-played it again for amusement, or just tossed it out to avoid anyone discovering it. Raza's decision to make the video would have had few if any consequences had it not entered the digital sphere. Unfortunately, Raza recorded his video on the cusp of a new era of media production and circulation.

Consider how the conditions of production have changed since 2002. After Raza made the video and his schoolmates discovered it, they had to transfer it to a new format, upload it to the internet, and then find a way to circulate it. Today, the same video would already be in a format ready to be posted on multiple sharing platforms, and the ability to circulate it would only be a click away. Other than the higher resolution, however, the production quality of a video made by an adolescent today would be much the same. What has changed is the speed and ease with which one can now share videos and, as a result, the size of the potential audience for even the most quotidian forms of self-representation. In short, the space and time that once separated shooting and editing images from circulating them have practically disappeared. Photographs and videos meant for oneself or just a few friends can easily get out of one's control and persist over time. Simply put, broadcasting is now in everyone's reach. But what have we given up as a result?

Raza, who was already an awkward teen with few friends at school, experienced an intensification of bullying as a result of his video's circulation. In the short term, he gave up his privacy—his right to do something goofy and then move beyond it. In the long term, the circulation of the video also made it impossible for him to forget the incident. Even changing schools and moving did not free him from this one fleeting moment of adolescent awkwardness. Emotions are sticky, and shame is no exception. What is unique about shame, however, is that it is an emotion contingent on a witness. One feels shame in the face of another.[32] Because the video was on a continuous loop, Raza became permanently stuck in the shame and humiliation that are part and parcel of the adolescent experience.

For someone like Parsons, much more was at stake than a goofy video. Like so many other young women, she had inadvertently become a victim of child pornography. Despite attempts to move to a new school, the images followed her, and so did the social networks in which the images originated. Young women who are victims of image-based abuse often report that after they move, it is only a matter of time before they start to receive messages and texts from boys asking them to send compromising images or videos.[33] For some of these young women, suicide may appear to be the only certain means of escape. In the short term, these young women are robbed of their privacy; in the long term, at least some of them are robbed of their lives.

Children and adolescents who gain notoriety online, although their circumstances are different, do have one thing in common: an online archive containing documentation of one or more episodes of their early years. Raza was robbed of the ability to try on an identity or role (in this case, the identity or role of a Star Wars character) and further robbed of the ability to repress the incident or reimagine it in a tolerable manner as he grew older. For girls like Parsons, who conclude that only death can release them from the compromising photographs and videos of their bodies circulating online, the loss is much greater. These young women lose the ability to occupy the role of victim for only a fleeting time. Experimenting sexually is part of growing up, and for many girls, so is being sexually assaulted. (Among first-year college students, for example, 17 percent of women report having already experienced sexual contact by physical force or incapacitation).[34] In the past, however, neither young women's sexual experiments nor assaults against them were widely documented. Adolescent sex, consensual or not, was something typically confined to bedrooms, basements, and bush parties. While Polaroid cameras did enable some compromising images of sexual experiments and assaults to slip into circulation, these images were one-of-a-kind documents that had more in common with paintings than with the images now found on Snapchat or Instagram. Today, bad sex and adolescent rape are no longer single incidents but, increasingly, incidents that repeat themselves. While it is true that violent acts also frequently repeat themselves in survivors' minds for years after their occurrence, what is remembered is typically not exactly what happened but rather a reworking of the incident—what Freud called a screen memory. And this raises another critical question: What happens to screen memories in the age of screens?

Screen Memories in a Multiscreen Era

When Freud published "Screen Memories" ("Über Deckerinnerungen") in 1899, he had no way of knowing how ubiquitous screens would eventually become or the extent to which they would shape future experiences of childhood and adolescence. Given that Freud often referred to the optical media of his era, especially photography, in his writings, it may be tempting to assume that he was thinking about screens both as filters and as projection surfaces when he wrote this essay, but there is little evidence to support this conclusion.[35] Although the standard edition of Freud's works translates *Deckerinnerungen* as "screen memories," a literal translation would be "covering" or "concealing" memories.

Freud's essay outlines three different types of screen memories. The first are those that conceal a different event that happened at the same time. For example, one might recall a tree branch falling. Although the incident did happen, it is taking the place of another more significant event that happened during the same timeframe (e.g., being whacked over the head with a wooden spoon). In the second type, a later recollection replaces the memory of a childhood event. Since few people recall anything at all before the age of four or five, they frequently transpose a memory from a later period onto this earlier period. The third type, which Freud mentions only in passing, is the "retrogressive screen memory." Here, an earlier memory comes to represent a later concern.[36] What all three categories of screen memories suggest is that memories of childhood are especially malleable. Their purpose, according to Freud, has less to do with a documentary impulse than with a self-protective one. People remember their childhoods in order to assimilate experiences rather than to reproduce them in any accurate manner.

Freud never adequately explained why we forget most of our early childhood and distort much of the rest of our childhood and adolescent years, but he did recognize just how pervasive false memories are. In "Screen Memories," he notes that when a person recalls their childhood, they tend to see themselves in the middle of a scene, as an outside observer would see them: "It is evident that such a picture cannot be an exact repetition of the impression that was originally received. For the subject was then in the middle of the situation and was attending not to himself but to the external world." That we remember not from our own perspective, but as if we were watching our childhood go by, is evidence that the retained memory has been manufactured after the fact rather than having been preserved as an original impression. While it may appear that these memory-traces from childhood are "translated back into a plastic and visual form," there is compelling reason to believe that "no reproduction of the original impression has ever entered the subject's consciousness." As evidence to support this claim Freud observes, "Out of a number of childhood memories of significant experiences, all of them of similar distinctness and clarity, there will be some scenes which, when they are tested (for instance by the recollections of adults), turn out to have been falsified." However, they are not completely invented: "They are false in the sense that they have shifted an event to a place where it did not occur ... or they have merged two people into one or substituted one for the other, or the scenes as a whole give signs of being combinations of two separate experiences." While one might be inclined to chalk such slips up to error, Freud insists that something deeper is at work:

Simple inaccuracy of recollection does not play any considerable part here, in view of the high degree of sensory intensity possessed by the images and the efficiency of the function of memory in the young; close investigation shows rather that these falsifications of memory are tendentious; that is, that they serve the purposes of the repression and replacement of objectionable or disagreeable impressions. It follows, therefore, that these falsified memories too, must have originated at a period of life when it has become possible for conflicts of this kind and impulsions towards repression to have made a place for themselves in mental life far later, therefore, than the period to which their content belongs.[37]

While Freud at times appears to separate these falsified memories from other childhood memories, at one point in "Screen Memories" he goes so far as to suggest that all of our childhood memories are screen memories: "It may indeed be questioned whether we have any memories at all from our childhood: memories relating to our child-hood may be all that we possess. Our childhood memories show us our earliest years not as they were but as they appeared at the later periods when the memories were aroused. In these periods of arousal, the childhood memories did not, as people are accustomed to say, emerge; they were formed at that time. And a number of motives, with no concern for historical accuracy, had a part in forming them, as well as in the selection of the memories themselves."[38]

Although never explicitly stated, Freud's essay suggests that screen memories enable individuals to gain control of a period of their life when they otherwise possessed little agency. Given that children not only have historically found themselves on the margins of society (in that they are unable to vote or even make medical deci-sions for themselves) but also, until recently, have not had the means to document and circulate images of themselves, this idea is of great consequence. Freud appears to suggest that long before children were able to create, edit, and curate images of their lives, they were already doing so on a psychic level. In a sense, screen memories might be understood as providing a space where children could edit and take control of their lives from the earliest age. In a world where young people are not accorded the same rights as adults, one thing they could always do was selectively edit what they chose to remember or to forget about their childhood and adolescence. Phyllis Greenacre, one of the few psychoanalysts to write at length about screen memories after Freud, notes that such memories could serve as "a deflection of focus from an intolerable horror to something which is reassuringly innocuous and familiar."[39]

The concept of screen memories is not without controversy; it has faced challenges from within the psychoanalytic profession and from the field of psychology more broadly. Because evidence-based research has not yet shown that unpacking screen memories yields significant clinical results (and, in some camps, there is doubt about whether repression and screen memories exist at all), the concept has lost ground with practicing analysts. In a 2015 volume of essays on Freud's concept, the editors note that screen memories "are rarely today at the centre of analysts' interests."[40] Some of the contributors to the volume suggest that this lack of interest may be due to the fact that identifying screen memories does not appear to result in their diminishment.[41]

However, even if unpacking screen memories may have limited potential to resolve traumas, Freud's early writings on childhood remembering and forgetting remain relevant. First, he appears to have believed that even if our childhood memories are false or distorted, they do not pose a threat to our mental well-being; neither does one's mental well-being depend on recovering and correcting our memories. He appreciated that screen memories could enable a person to turn an intolerable horror into something innocuous and familiar. For example, Freud observed that his patients often recalled incidental events from their childhood (e.g., the loss or damage to a toy) during periods when serious and tragic events occurred.[42] Some neuroscientists have found evidence that supports this idea, showing that memories appear to be continually updated.[43] But in an age when electronic screens are ubiquitous, will screen memories, like forgetting, become the exception rather than the rule? If so, will we lose the ability to turn the intolerable horrors and simply shameful incidents that are so often part of growing up into innocuous and familiar fragments of memory? Are we losing the ability to create screen memories—that small but significant site of agency that has always been afforded to young people? Is this the high-stakes tradeoff for finally gaining the ability to engage in both self-representation and broadcasting?

In the process of trading screen memories for screens, the stakes are much higher for children and adolescents than for adults, and are much higher for some young people than for others. Like earlier child celebrities, some of today's children and teens whose lives are excessively documented will probably emerge unscathed, while others will not. The future of someone like Gavin, who has circulated as a meme since he was two years old, will rest largely on whether a reasonable effort is made to mitigate the potentially negative or exploitative effects of celebrity and exposure.

For victims of cyberbullying, the consequences are much more profound. Ghyslain Raza, for example, would have been better served by screen memories than screens. Raza will never be able to forget his awkward fifteenth year. Type his name into any search engine, and multiple versions of the *Star Wars Kid* video will appear. Raza has never had an opportunity to turn his fleeting moment of goofy abandon into a screen memory, and he never will. With the documentary trace of the event still in circulation over fifteen years later, there is no possibility of effectively concealing the event or letting a later recollection stand in for the event, or rewriting the event through the lens of his adult experiences. Although Raza's situation was unique—both because it occurred when social media had just been developed and because it garnered more online and traditional media attention than any internet meme since—any child or adolescent growing up now has the potential to become another Raza. Thankfully, not all young people are bullied online, as Raza was; but when they are in their mid-twenties, they may no longer be able to rely on the screen memories that have traditionally afforded relief from the feelings of shame, humiliation, and fear that are invariably part of growing up. We appear to be hardwired to distort and conceal the most intolerable memories of childhood. But we are now living in a world where this protective impulse is increasingly threatened by the screens upon which so much of our lives and early development unfold.

When Tagged Subjects Leave Home

F or most people, leaving home—not simply their family home, but also the community where they grew up—is a pivotal moment. Not everyone has something to escape or a pressing need to reinvent themselves, but many people do. For some people, leaving home is synonymous with breaking away from tradition. For others, it is a way to escape an abusive environment, transcend their social class, or come out. In short, people leave home for multiple reasons and sometimes as a matter of survival. Leaving home, however, is not what it was in the past. Indeed, one of the most notable material consequences of the demise of forgetting may be the profound change it is having on the once taken-for-granted act of leaving home.

As social media networks expand, along with access to information about remote locations, physically leaving home may be easier now than ever before. Young people have new tools at their disposal to research their futures lives. Someone whose dream of attending a college on the other side of the country or the other side of the world, who might formerly have been thwarted by lack of information, can spend hours online researching potential schools and scholarship opportunities and even chatting with admissions counselors. This may be one reason why the out-of-state student population at public universities in the United States more than doubled between 1986 and 2016.[1] But choosing a far-flung college is not the only option available to young people who wish to move away. Online platforms from Craigslist to SpareRoom also make it easy for adolescents to connect with new friends, potential roommates, and jobs in other locations nationwide and around the world. If a young person wishes to escape their small town or suburb, they no longer have to face the once daunting prospect of getting on a bus or train and showing up in a new city with nowhere to go but a local youth hostel. In the twenty-first century, they can carefully plan their escape and even set up a new life and social network long before they arrive in their desired destination.

Despite these conditions, however, other aspects of leaving home—especially the act of executing a complete and radical break with the past—have become more difficult. Just as the decline of forgetting has different stakes for different demographics, the difficulty of breaking away from the past affects different people in profoundly different ways. In a sense, we are now all tagged subjects—subjects whose movements can not only be easily tracked but whose past selves can be recalled and put back into circulation at any time. A person wanting to leave home and leave the past behind now faces two new and unique obstacles. First, there is the problem of slipping under the radar in the present. And second, there is the problem of preventing the past from attaching itself to the present. The structure of social media networks, facial recognition technologies, automated tagging, and emerging augmented reality applications are all converging in ways that may soon turn the experience of leaving home into a distant memory. But how did we reach this point?

To appreciate how we arrived at our current situation, one needs to consider two histories. The first is a history of tracking devices and how these devices, once used primarily on nonhuman animals, evolved over the course of the past century and have recently become embraced by human animals. The other is also a history of tagging, but it is the much more recent history of photo tagging. If it is becoming increasingly difficult to leave the past behind, this is largely due to the convergence of these two tagging histories—one focused on hardware, and the other focused on data.

Social Networks That Move with Us

For most of human existence, geography determined the limits of social relations. Social networks were defined by location and stretched only as far as a person could walk, paddle, or sail. Our social networks were only as enduring as our memories, which are invariably fallible. Since the invention of writing, new media have been alleviating at least some of the burden once carried by our memories. From written letters to telegraphs to telephones, these social media of earlier eras helped us sustain relationships at a distance and over time.

A number of media theorists have explored the idea that our media profoundly affect our social interactions and relations. In his book *No Sense of Place* (1986), Joshua Meyrowitz, drawing heavily on the work of Erving Goffman and Marshall McLuhan, observed that electronic media "have altered the significance of time and space for social interaction." Meyrowitz echoed some of the claims Neil Postman had made a few years earlier, in *The Disappearance of Childhood.* Like Postman, Meyrowitz associated electronic media with a collapse of physical boundaries (at the time, electronic media referred primarily to radio, television, and telephones and, to a lesser extent, emerging digital media such as home computers). Worlds once confined to adults, he claimed, were becoming accessible to children. Along with the collapse of physical boundaries, which he compared to living in a house without rooms or walls, Meyrowitz argued that social behaviors and relationships were shifting. For example, in the face-to-face world, other than during special occasions (e.g., family weddings), it is rarely necessary to navigate multiple audiences at the same time (e.g., family, friends, and colleagues). Like Goffman, Meyrowitz pointed out that we are all social actors who play different roles on different social stages, and that some of these roles take years to perfect. Electronic media disrupt this clear boundary by rearranging the social forums we occupy in new ways, creating what he called "combined situations." In electronically mediated social situations, for example, we may encounter many different types of audiences simultaneously, while also losing the context and social cues that make it possible for us to respond to these situations. "The combined situations of electronic media are relatively lasting and inescapable," he contended, "and they therefore have a much greater effect on social behavior." Meyrowitz drifted away from Postman's earlier argument, however, in that he was less concerned with the content of new media than with the ways in which they were changing our "sense of place" or lack of it. He saw electronic media as affecting us not primarily through their content but by altering "the 'situational geography' of social life."[2]

In many respects, Meyrowitz's predictions were accurate. He recognized the extent to which new media, including emerging digital media, were eroding once clearly defined boundaries between specific types of social spaces (e.g., the family home and college dorm), making it difficult for people to step into stable and fixed context-specific social roles. What Meyrowitz could not have easily predicted in the mid-1980s was that by the early 2000s, face-to-face interactions (such as those experienced at a family wedding) would also become highly mediated by electronic media. After all, few weddings or even funerals now go by without participants wandering off, so to speak, to interact with friends in online social environments. Such events are also increasingly documented and even live-streamed, to invite in anyone who cannot be physically present. Meyrowitz also did not foresee the collapse of time and, with it, the blurring of past and present social networks.

In earlier electronic cultures, the boundaries of the family home were partially breached by technologies such as the telephone, radio, and television, which provided access to other people and places.[3] Now, in the twenty-first century, we are living in a world where not only have the walls of the family home been dismantled, so to speak, but also all the contents of the family home—the old photo albums and home movies and, worse yet, the embarrassing stories and unwelcome memories—have gained the ability to be put back into circulation and even to exist on a continuous loop.

Older media technologies, even though they also had a profound impact on social relationships, did not threaten our ability to sever social networks when and if we sought to do so. In the past, letters could go unanswered, telegraphs could be ignored, and telephones could ring without being answered. A person could choose to stop forwarding their new address or decide to delist their telephone number to deflect unwelcome callers from the past. Without much effort, in the world of analogue media, we could control with whom we remained in touch. Our addresses and phone numbers functioned as identification markers, but we controlled who did and did not have access to this information and who could find us in the present. We were generally as visible and connected as we chose to be and were free to put whatever distance we wished between the past and the present.

In the twenty-first century, this has changed. Moving away no longer necessarily entails losing touch, and this holds true whether we make an effort to remain connected to our family and friends or not. In many respects, this newfound connectivity is comforting. Consider the profound differences that separate the experiences of twenty-first century migrants from the millions of people who fled Europe during World War II. Western journalists routinely document today's migrants crawling out of overcrowded rubber dinghies and leaky boats to call and text family and friends left behind in countries across North Africa and the Middle East. Since 2015, photographs of a new generation of texting migrants have become ubiquitous. So too have stories of migrants blogging and tweeting about their journeys across Europe. In sharp contrast to the experience of migrants in the 1940s or 1950s, and even the 1980s, family members left behind can now stay in constant touch with their sons and daughters and even track their footsteps across Europe and around the world using tracking apps, such as iPhone's Find My Friends. But for some migrants, bringing social networks with them has come with unexpected consequences. Those left behind remain present 24/7, and the constant barrage of messages, photographs, and videos from loved ones in refugee camps and war zones can make it difficult to recover from their trauma, even as they move on physically.[4] It is not only migrants, however, who are on the move and bringing their social networks with them.

Consider the far more routine ritual of leaving home to attend university. Leaving home used to be simple. When I left the rural community where I grew up—after years of anticipating the moment and worrying that I might not survive to see the day—I made a more or less clean break with the past. I did stay in touch with three or four friends from high school during my first year of university, but by the time I was a sophomore, I had lost touch with virtually everyone from my high school and community. At the end of my first year, I decided to transfer to a new university. Again, the break was complete. By the time I applied to graduate school four years later, I no longer had the phone numbers or addresses of anyone I had known in high school or my first year of university. In my late teens and early twenties my social networks were constantly in flux. People came and went as I tried on different locations, lifestyles, and identities. The fact that I could form intense relationships, both romantic and nonromantic, and move on just as quickly was liberating. The ability to execute a radical break with the past, especially from the rural community where I had grown up, also made it much easier (in an era before high school gay–straight alliance clubs and gay marriage legislation) to come out as queer.

Today, someone from a similar background moving away under comparable circumstances with a desire to reinvent themselves would face obstacles that I did not encounter. In the past, staying in touch required at least some effort. When I left for university, for example, I had to exchange phone numbers and addresses with the few friends with whom I hoped to stay in touch. Today's college students arrive on campus with many more connections. Their established social networks move away with them. These networks typically include not only close friends but also distant acquaintances from high school and even middle and elementary school, as well as relatives and family friends and hundreds of other people they have met along the way. Adolescents today travel into the future with a constant stream of images and updates from their place of origin. They are continuously called back into the past. To be clear, this may not be entirely negative. For some young people, social media can help them manage life transitions, including the transition from home to college.[5] If they do wish to sever established social networks, however, they now need to do much more than simply get up and leave.

To leave home (both physically and socially), one must also "prune" one's online social networks by deactivating established social media accounts or at least blocking certain people from the past. However, blocking only a few people (say, a high school bully or insignificant family friend) may be inadequate. If other people in one's network are still connected to people who have been banished, so to speak, they may still remain present by proxy. Over many years of teaching introductory courses in media studies, I have frequently asked my undergraduate students to discuss how they grapple with this dilemma. While many of the students either assume there is no way to execute a clean break with the past or simply have no desire to do so, each year I meet at least a few students who have gone to extraordinary lengths to accomplish this once simple task. Not surprisingly, these students typically have a compelling reason to want to put at least some distance between their past and present lives. Some of these young people identify as lesbian, gay, or transgender but come from a place where there is still limited tolerance, at best, for such identities. Some come from rural communities and have arrived in New York City with dreams of reinventing themselves as artists, musicians, or writers. Some are young women desperate to escape the destinies that have been inscribed upon them since birth. As an example, consider just one of these young people.

Kevin, an aspiring film critic from a small town in upstate New York, which he cynically depicts as a place best known for its high population of murderers (the town is home to a maximum-security prison), is one of the few students I have encountered who has attempted to completely "kill" his old data subject and start anew. "By my second year," he told me, "my [Facebook] stream was getting really weird. I had my new friends from New York posting about queer performance art and these guys from my high school posting about dirt biking in a gravel pit and tagging me in photographs from high school. I needed to move on." To "move on," Kevin took the radical measure of deactivating all his social media accounts and opening new accounts under a pseudonym, with a new email address. His experiment, as it turned out, was only semi-successful. Even with his new accounts and new identity, he continued to receive friend suggestions pointing back to the social networks he had attempted to sever. Then, somewhat impulsively, he made the mistake of adding back into his network just one old friend with whom he was still in touch. That decision opened a floodgate of connection requests from his former acquaintances. Although no one knew who he was (since he was now using a new name and avatar), their single mutual connection triggered algorithms that suggested further connections. Despite all his efforts, Kevin was unable to fully separate from his old social networks and was not optimistic about ever realizing a complete break with the past. "My mom has this hilarious high school yearbook. She takes it out every few years and laughs and then throws in back into a box in the basement. I wish I could do that, but I can't," he said. "I still get tagged—I mean, the old me gets tagged—in pictures from high school that guys I knew then post online. I guess that Kevin is out there for good, and I just have to live with him and all those people he was trying to escape."

Kevin's dilemma clearly illustrates two unique obstacles to leaving home in the twenty-first century. First, social media platforms move with us across space and time. Where moving from place to place once made it difficult to maintain social relations, with the spread of social media platforms such as Facebook, geographical distance no longer poses much of a threat. Second, tagging, and especially the automated tagging of photographs, is profoundly changing how the past is brought into the present.

A Short History of Tagged Subjects

To appreciate what it means to be a tagged subject, like Kevin, it is helpful to briefly consider the history of tagging. Until recently, tagging was a material practice reserved almost exclusively for non-human rather than human animals.

Take, for example, the history of tagging birds. For centuries, people in northern regions wondered what happened to birds each winter. Did they fly off to a warmer place, change into a different species, or hibernate like snakes and frogs? The migratory patterns of birds were a mystery great enough to attract the attention of scholars from Aristotle to Homer to Pliny the Elder. In the *History of Animals,* Aristotle claimed what while some birds do migrate, others, including doves, swallows, and kites, simply burrow into holes.[6] Well into the twentieth century, bird migration continued to baffle biologists. Systematic attempts to track birds began in the early nineteenth century, when biologists started to catch birds and tag them by putting a small band around one leg.[7] This method, however, yielded limited data because only a small percentage of birds were ever rediscovered. It wasn't until the mid-twentieth century that biologists finally discovered a better approach, using telemetry. Telemetry originated in the nineteenth century as a wired technology and was refined as a wireless surveillance tool during World War II. After the war, telemetry relied on radio waves to transmit information about things and eventually living creatures from remote locations. A precursor to current GPS-based technologies, it allowed biologists to obtain data at a distance and, more importantly, to track creatures on the move.[8]

Assuming that birds, fish, and even primates do not have any understanding of privacy and therefore no need to maintain it, efforts to tag and track the movements of nonhuman animals have generally remained unchallenged. Since the mid-twentieth century, this practice has also resulted in reams of data on where animals go and what they do throughout the year. But tagging wild animals represents only one type of tagging—one primarily focused on generating scientific knowledge. Since the 1990s, tagging not only has taken new forms but has come to be driven by motivations that extend well beyond the desire to generate knowledge.

In the mid-1990s, veterinarians started routinely implanting microchips in domestic animals, such as cats and dogs. These small electronic chips, inserted just under the skin, contain identifying information about the pet. While pets had previously been marked in other ways (e.g., with tags or tattoos), microchipping, which cost only $15 to $45 per pet at the time, was widely accepted as a more effective way to identify pets who wandered away from home.[9] As a result, hundreds of thousands of responsible pet-owners who would never have dreamt of microchipping their children, spouses, or elderly parents started to microchip their cats and dogs. Although one could not yet track one's cat prowling around the neighborhood in real time (this is now possible using GPS-based technologies, including affordable trackers that clip on to a pet's collar), microchip programs offered some assurance that if Whiskers went missing, he or she would be more likely to be found and returned. But the move to microchipping household pets did something else. Many people consider their pets to be part of the family. Unlike the wild hawks, pheasants, otters, and wolves that biologists have been tagging and tracking for decades, pets live with us and even eat in our kitchens and sleep in our beds. The acceptance of microchipping pets signaled a shift toward a broader acceptance of tracking, if not yet of people, at least of living creatures we care deeply about.[10] In other words, as we started to chip our pets, electronic tracking moved from an exclusively data-driven practice (one focused on gathering information for research purposes) to an affective one (one focused on keeping track of beloved pets). It is no surprise, then, that by the early 2000s, some people began to think that microchipping human loved ones might also be a good idea.

In 2002, a family from southern Florida made headlines around the world when they elected to have microchips implanted in their arms. The decision was driven by the family's fourteen-year-old son, Derek, who persuaded his parents that the implants were a potentially life-saving security device. The family members later explained to CBS News that Derek's father had a lot of health problems, and they felt safer knowing that in an emergency, first responders would be able to identify him.[11] Despite their seemingly good intentions, at the time, the family's decision to chip themselves was questioned by some medical ethicists and ridiculed by the media and the general public. Shortly after the Jacobs family went public about their decision, the journalist and novelist Lev Grossman, then the lead technology writer for *Time* magazine, published a cheeky article on the family under the headline, "Meet the Chipsons." Other people, including the privacy expert Richard Smith, skeptically wondered if the family's decision to get chipped was simply a publicity stunt.[12]

Despite FDA approval of the VeriChip implanted into members of the Jacobs family, microchips for humans have never been widely embraced. Over fifteen years later, the practice—and even the idea of the practice—continues to receive a chilly reception.[13] This is likely because science fiction narratives such as *Robocop* and *Neuromancer* have reinforced the idea that microchipping humans is synonymous with a loss of privacy, individuality, agency, and control. But given the persistent resistance to the idea of microchipping, how do we account for the fact that many people in the world allow themselves to be tagged and tracked in other ways, often by choice?

Shortly after the Jacobs family was voluntarily chipped, an unrelated technological development made the tagging of humans far more pervasive but also far less obvious. After decades of development in a military context and heavy regulation, GPS-enabled devices were finally authorized for nonmilitary use, creating new possibilities for civilians to track each other, too.[14] As GPS-enabled smartphones were launched by mobile phone manufacturers, parents were identified as an obvious target market. These phone models were costly, and a parent often had to pay every time they logged in to spy on their child at a distance. Nevertheless, these devices found a market, for two reasons: demand from parents who had long dreamt of being able to track their children, and a willingness on the part of children and teens to voluntarily carry a cellphone wherever they went.[15] As Apple iPhones flooded the market, and apps such as Find My Friends (which allowed people to locate friends who agreed to share their location) became commonplace, the cost of tracking-equipped phones plummeted, and many people began to track their loved ones day and night. For children too young to carry their own phones, other GPS-based devices appeared on the market, often disguised as watches or cute clip-on accessories shaped like flowers or robots.[16] This change, rather than a deeper aversion to electronic tracking, is arguably what slowed the move to microchip humans. However, GPS-equipped devices were not the only things causing humans to become tagged subjects during the first two decades of the twenty-first century. Many of us also started to tag ourselves and each other in photographs. It is photo tagging, rather than tracking devices or implanted chips, that may ultimately pose the greatest obstacle to anyone who wishes to move away and not remain tethered to the past.

The Origins of Photo Tagging

In the mid-2000s, Joshua Schachter, founder of the website Delicious (originally del.icio.us), adopted the tagging metaphor to help introduce nonexperts to the concept of metadata. Shortly thereafter, "tagging," both the term and the practice, was also adopted by the photo-sharing site Flickr.[17]

Metadata is the term used for data that describes other data. In the analogue world, metadata was something generally of concern only to specialists (e.g., library catalogers). This doesn't mean that regular folks hadn't been using metadata all along. A penciled note on the back of an old family photograph indicating who is in the photograph and where and when it was taken is an example of metadata. Of course, the note on the back of a photograph of your aunt sitting on the dock at the cottage was metadata that only you would likely ever see. As digital data continued to proliferate in the early 2000s—largely due to the popularity of social media platforms that enabled anyone to publish their writing, post images, or upload videos—it became clear that a radically new approach to metadata was required. Accumulating digital photographs was both simple and inexpensive, but searching and retrieving such images on the basis of their content was not. As people's personal photograph collections started to grow at a much more rapid pace than they had in the past (largely due to the fact that development costs were no longer an obstacle), retrievability became an increasingly pressing problem.[18] One solution to the problem of how to manage the vast amounts of content circulating online was to put metadata tools into users' hands—in short, to turn everyone into an indexer. What happened next was both a savvy way to address a growing crisis in information management and a deeply democratizing gesture. The hope was that the challenge of organizing all this data could be made more manageable by enabling everyone to add metadata to digital artifacts, and by enabling this metadata to be visible to others, even strangers. Perhaps because the concept of metadata is somewhat obscure, the easier-to-understand concept of tagging was soon adopted. But there was at least one profound difference between earlier metadata projects and the one now unfolding on media sharing platforms. Metadata had historically relied on established taxonomies for classifying data (e.g., Library of Congress subject headings); digital tagging, by contrast, relied on what the information architect Thomas Vander Wal first described in 2004 as "folksonomies."[19]

On the surface, nothing could sound less threatening and less ominous than a folksonomy. The word conjures up an image of friendly folks coming together to make sense of an information-rich world from their own perspectives. At first, this was essentially how folksonomies operated. By definition, folksomonies are composed of freely selectable keywords or tags that can be attached to any information resource. On sites like Flickr, early tagging efforts often simply entailed people adding basic information such as the names of people, places, or events to their photographs. Of course, the beauty of a folksonomy is that people are also free to attach more esoteric tags to their photographs and, over time, many people did. "The information you get [through tags]," admitted Schachter, "is always going to be somewhat imperfect and fuzzy. But a bunch of people doing 'okay' tagging may actually have a higher net value than an authoritative organization telling you how information should be organized."[20]

In retrospect, it seems likely that people quickly began tagging photographs on media sharing sites such as Flickr in the mid-2000s because it was fun and easy, and because most users considered it to be entirely innocuous. If someone tagged their sister or a friend, it was assumed to be a useful way to guarantee that they could retrieve the photograph later or that others could identify the people in the photograph in the months, years, or decades to come. Digital photo tagging started as an extension of a practice—writing a note on the back of a photograph—that was already familiar and widespread. But what happened next was not a mere continuation of the time-honored practice of adding metadata to images.

When Flickr became popular in the mid- to late 2000s, photo tagging did not feel like an invasion of privacy or a threat to forgetting. At the time, most Flickr users would have been shocked to discover that their voluntary labor (tagging photographs of friends and family) might have broader consequences. Only later did we discover that these users were helping to lay the groundwork for a world in which tagging would no longer rely on the fallible memories of humans but would be conducted by intelligent machines. Some people, however, had already figured this out. The journalist Clay Shirky observed in 2005, "The strategy of tagging—free-form labeling, without regard to categorical constraints—seems like a recipe for disaster, but as the Web has shown us, you can extract a surprising amount of value from big messy data sets."[21] Shirky's prediction would prove to be eerily accurate, but it was ultimately not Flickr that would drive the next development.

By 2010, Facebook had already surpassed Flickr and all other online companies to become the world's largest repository of digital photographs. Early on, tagging on the popular social media platform was similar to what had been established on competing sites, such as Flickr. But with an estimated 100 million tags being added to photographs on Facebook every day, the company was well positioned to start rolling out its first experiment in automated tagging.[22] It was also around this time that consumers began to abandon their old flip phones and replace them with new camera phones, resulting in a spike in the number of photos taken and circulated. The market research firm InfoTrends estimated that from 2010 to 2015, the number of photos taken worldwide tripled, rising from 350 billion to 1 trillion per year.[23] The convergence between photo tagging and the widespread adoption of camera phones would have far-reaching impacts, specifically on the development of automated facial recognition.

Facebook's practice of automated tagging (auto-tagging) was initially collaborative; the platform would simply make suggestions about how a user might like to tag a photograph. If you had already tagged your best friend, Mira, in many photographs, Facebook would suggest tagging Mira in a new photo if its facial recognition system identified the new face as hers. Many Facebook users welcomed the suggested tags. Rather than having to spend several minutes tagging group photos, you could now share some of the tagging labor with Facebook's semi-intelligent robots. While the company's engineers were partly responsible for perfecting the auto-tagging feature, like it or not, so were Facebook's users. Facebook not only had the largest storehouse of digital photographs, but thanks to users' early enthusiasm for tagging, it had also amassed the largest storehouse of tagged photographs in the world. This combination of assets laid the groundwork for the facial recognition technologies that are now compromising our ability to control our visibility in the present and the past.

Although it is difficult to pinpoint the precise moment when photo tagging started to be viewed as something that could compromise individual privacy rights, early warning signs started to appear in 2011. In the summer of that year, a German data protection supervisor warned that the platform's automated photo-tagging feature could violate European privacy laws.[24] At the same time, U.S. courts were beginning to grapple with Facebook's new facial recognition tools. In 2012, Facebook briefly pulled the plug on its auto-tagging function. At the same time, however, it purchased Face.com, an Israeli company that Facebook had previously hired to help develop its facial recognition software.[25] During the following year, Facebook worked to improve its facial recognition feature, and by early 2013, all Facebook users, at least those living in the United States, were automatically reenrolled in the platform's new and improved automated tagging experiment.

Since then, Facebook, along with other big players in technology, including Google, have continued to refine their facial recognition technologies. These companies have accomplished something that promises to change our visibility not only in the present but also in the past. This is where the next episode in the history of tagging begins.

No Longer Just Another Face in the Crowd

As facial recognition technologies became smarter, two things happened, and they happened very quickly. To begin with, crowd-based facial recognition became ubiquitous. Special investigators are no longer the only people who have the tools needed to scan large crowds and accurately identify people. Since most of our faces have now been tagged, the chance of making a correct match—even in a photograph of a crowd—have drastically increased over the past decade. This type of facial recognition has received considerable attention in the media, largely because a person can now easily be auto-tagged in a photograph they had no idea was being taken. For example, if a father snaps a picture of his child on a busy street corner and then posts the image to Facebook, the once anonymous faces in the background may also be tagged. People may find themselves tagged in a complete stranger's private moments—a phenomenon that also evidently makes everyone's whereabouts far more visible.[26] But street scenes are not the only places one can be tagged. Activists face the potentially troubling prospect of being tagged in photographs taken at protests. While there have been some attempts to circumvent facial recognition technologies (e.g., by developing clothing items and even face paint designed to confuse algorithms), the potential of being spotted at a demonstration is much greater than ever before.[27] The stakes may be especially high for young people, who are more likely to attend protest events and to put their bodies on the front lines. However, automated facial recognition technologies have another effect that is not about space (e.g., being spotted in a crowd), but rather about time and history.

Early commercial facial recognition software did a relatively good job of identifying one's friends or family members in the present but could not always identify the same people in older photographs, especially those that had been scanned, uploaded, and posted online. As facial recognition technologies improve, tagging of old photographs is becoming more accurate.[28] Old digital photographs, and even digitized photographs from older printed sources (e.g., high school yearbooks), can now be tagged. For many people, especially those interested in family history, the development of tools that can automatically identify people in older photographs will no doubt be a welcome development. But what about reluctant tagged subjects like my student Kevin, whom I introduced earlier in the chapter?

For anyone who wishes to leave home and create a comfortable, if not complete, distance between their present life and their past life, facial recognition technologies pose a major obstacle. To move on, they must effectively "manage" the person they left behind, who is now liable to be automatically tagged in photographs—even those taken twenty years ago. While this may not sound devastating, consider the analogue equivalent. You are enjoying a regular day at work when a UPS delivery arrives, and your colleagues open the box. The box contains five old high school yearbooks and a dozen family photo albums. Suddenly, your coworkers are all poring over mortifying pictures of you from your bar mitzvah in seventh grade and asking you about the mullet you had around the time you were the president of your high school science club. While this may sound absurd, in fact, this horrifying possibility is now in reach as facial recognition moves beyond the present and reaches into the past to identify and pull up previously untagged images. For anyone born before the 1990s, the convergence of the past and the present will be minimized by the fact that their childhoods unfolded in the era of analogue photography (unless those earlier photographs have been digitized). For people born since then, however, the situation is profoundly different, since there is a higher likelihood that their lives were documented in digital rather than analogue media from the beginning.

The problem of leaving home in the age of social media, then, is twofold. First, there is the simple fact that we live in an era when our social networks are likely to travel with us to our next location. Second, our past selves can be pulled into our present social networks by means of facial recognition. Defenders of automated photo tagging, which include social media companies whose profits are linked to facial recognition technologies, are quick to point out that users are not helpless. As Facebook likes to remind users, if you do not want your own photographs to be automatically tagged or tagged by others, you can adjust your settings so the tagged images do not appear in your feed. Of course, you cannot in fact stop others from tagging you or entirely shut down the platform's automated tagging function. Similarly, on Instagram, the onus is on users who do not wish to be tagged to control, if not prevent, themselves from being tagged either automatically or by other users. However, anyone who has ever spent time on a social media platform knows that these rules are constantly changing, and controlling how and when you are tagged can feel overwhelming and even hopeless. For someone like Kevin, who just wants to put the past behind him, the burden of managing his past self—and keeping his old friends and acquaintances at a distance—is an ongoing project and a distraction that a young man attempting to craft a new identity in a new place should not have to be burdened with.

Winners and Losers

In the twentieth century, science fiction writers offered versions of a dystopian future where humans roamed the world with microchips implanted in their brains. In the end, however, the quotidian and seemingly innocuous photo album, not the microchip, may ultimately be what renders us fully visible in the present and the past and threatens our ability to both forget and be forgotten. The winners here are self-evident: technology companies and specifically those with major storehouses of data, including Facebook and Google.[29] But who are the losers?

I would like to suggest that the people who have the most to lose from these current technological developments are those who have the most to gain from putting at least some distance between themselves and the past. While many people have good reason to remain deeply connected to the past, others benefit from leaving the past behind. For many queer youth, the ability to leave the past behind remains essential. Other experiences—the experience of growing up poor, for example—may also require people to "reinvent" themselves. One may not need to cut off old friends and family entirely, but one's social mobility may require a strategic bracketing off of one's past. The people who will pay the highest price for our arrival in a data-rich world where not only photographs but eventually other sorts of physical objects are tagged with myriad layers of data, then, are those who previously had the most to gain from being able to take flight and reinvent themselves in another place and time.[30] To be clear, this is not to suggest that tagging and facial recognition are entirely detrimental. As encounters with earlier technologies demonstrate, users' creative, imaginative, and often politically motivated redeployments of technologies cannot be underestimated. But history also suggests that encounters with new media technologies are frequently shaped by one's identity and physical location.[31] People who have never had the privilege of romanticizing home—those whose survival may even depend on taking leave and putting some distance between the present and past—seem likely to be more at risk of ending up on the losing side of this technological equation.

5 In Pursuit of Digital Disappearance

D isappearance was never easy—not even in the age of print. Take, for example, the story of Danielle Collobert. The experimental French writer reportedly had so many regrets about her first book, published in 1961, that she attempted to retrieve all the copies in circulation. Like many writers, she had a desire to forget her first book—but to do so, she needed to ensure that everyone else would also forget about it.[1] After all, one's ability to forget depends on other people's willingness not to remind us of the very thing we hope to erase. For Collobert, erasure was something she believed she could take into her own hands and ultimately did.

Now imagine if Collobert had been born in the late 1990s, rather than in 1940, and had started publishing (or self-publishing) online. Born into a different era, she might have had considerably more early work in circulation, perhaps including juvenilia, but retrieving it would have been an entirely different story. Unlike a writer from an earlier period, who might have known that there were only three hundred, or three thousand, copies of their first book in circulation, an aspiring writer of today who posts their poems on Instagram may have no idea where their work has traveled. One might argue that not much has changed from Collobert to Instagram since Collobert did not, in fact, manage to destroy all the copies of her first book (at least one copy evidently survived, since the book was posthumously reissued).[2] Nevertheless, at least one thing has changed, and it is precisely what we once took for granted: the ability to know how many copies of a text are in circulation and the related ability to at least imagine taking them back. Of course, first books are not the only things one might want to erase.

In a conversation about the subject of my book, a colleague confessed to me that he understood precisely why digital erasure might be desirable. My colleague, it turns out, once went through what he glibly describes as a "porn phase." At the time, he was a young gay man who couldn't quite make ends meet. Acting in a porn film was a fast and easy way to make money without interrupting his studies. Years later, when he was walking through the foyer of a hotel at an international conference in his field, an older man approached him, insisting they must know each other—perhaps from a graduate seminar or past conference. Then, the stranger realized that my colleague was familiar from another context entirely. "Oh, you're the skateboarder!" he exclaimed. This was not the first time my colleague had been "outed." He explained that in his youth, he had skateboarded his way into gay porn fame, and well over a decade later, his contribution to the world of gay porn continued to circulate online and attract a large number of viewers. Fortunately, my colleague has managed to incorporate his past endeavors into his present life with relative ease (after all, he is a queer theory professor working on a progressive campus in New York City). One can imagine that had he chosen to work in a different field (e.g., politics, law enforcement, or K–12 education), his history might be cause for much greater concern. He might urgently want to forget it and have it forgotten by others. But if my colleague did want to erase his "porn phase," would it be possible?

Whether hoping to distance oneself from past postings of poetry or porn, in the digital world, the process of erasing data is no simple matter. As a result, forgetting and being forgotten are also a challenge. While there may be ways to increase the chances of achieving some form of digital disappearance, it seems unlikely that anything more than partial disappearance is possible.

The real reason why digital disappearance is something we are unlikely to achieve now or at any point in the future is not simply that we all live in the presence of our digital footprints and digital shadows. The individual desire for disappearance is also in conflict with both technological and economic agendas. On the surface, permanently deleting an aspiring poet's work or a young scholar's porn film would seem to have no impact on the future of technology. Likewise, the aspiring poet's work and even the porn film might have no or only limited potential to generate income. But all of these small bits of data, each of which generates more data, hold considerable value. They are drivers of both technology and the twenty-first-century economy. This means that forgetting—that once taken-for-granted built-in resource that all humans possessed—is now being pitted against the interests of technology companies and, more broadly, any company that seeks to use data to optimize its products or services. The real struggle is no longer one between forgetting and memory, but rather between forgetting and the rising value of data, even data that once carried no intrinsic value whatsoever. For a variety of reasons, children and adolescents are affected by this shift in significantly different ways and to a different degree than adults.

Digital Space, Digital Time, and the Psychosocial Moratorium

The psychoanalyst Erik Erikson believed that youth ought to be granted a bit of slack, since adolescence and even young adulthood are times of intense personal exploration. As we saw in Chapter 2, Erikson noted that most cultures have historically granted young people a psychosocial moratorium, when they were exempt from the consequences of their experiences. Before the spread of social media platforms and the unprecedented documentation of childhood and adolescence that we are now witnessing, a higher percentage of youth did have the freedom to experiment, mess up, and move on with few consequences (though, I caution, the ability to do so has always varied depending on one's race, class, and gender). Digital media, as I suggested earlier, have already largely eroded this psychosocial moratorium. But could it be reinstated through some sort of data erasure process? Some attempts have been made to institute such a process legislatively, but digital media practices constantly undermine such attempts.

Many people certainly believe that children and youth should be able to make mistakes without the world watching. Indeed, a number of nations around the world (but not the United States) have laws prohibiting the publication of young offenders' names in the media.[3] The logic is that minors should be able to err and move on to adult life unscathed by their youthful mistakes in judgment. These laws reflect a tacit societal understanding that young people should be allowed some sort of moratorium on consequences. There is now growing support for legislation that would grant young people similar special rights in relation to data erasure, but these efforts face considerable challenges.[4]

One of the challenges of the data erasure legislation introduced in the European Union is that it relies on the distinction between public and private citizens. Article 17 of the EU General Data Protection Regulation requires data controllers (entities that gather data) to balance an individual subject's right to be forgotten against "public interest" in the data when considering whether to grant a request to erase data.[5] On the one hand, this makes perfect sense. If your next-door neighbor holds an orgy, one of the guests posts some photographs online, and the neighbor requests that they be deleted, that seems like a legitimate request. There is no reason for you to know how your neighbor chooses to pass their leisure time. On the other hand, if your next-door neighbor happens to be the mayor and invites other public officials to the party, access to this information could be important, since it may tell you something about your mayor's poor judgment or abuse of power. But this raises two important questions. In the digital world, how does one separate public figures from private citizens? And what about children and adolescents who become public figures?

As social media sites have proliferated, determining who is and is not a public figure has grown increasingly difficult. The medium itself has the ability to turn private persons into public figures, and to do so at a staggeringly fast rate. This is precisely what happened to Ghyslain Raza, who was turned into the Star Wars Kid seemingly overnight after his video was posted online. For Raza, becoming an internet meme was a devastating experience. Had he been born in France rather than in Québec, however, and had he remained there as an adult, would he now be able to request that every past mention of his name in relation to the Star Wars Kid be deindexed, so it no longer appears in online searches? Could he request that every version of the *Star Wars Kid* video, including the multiple remakes by "fans," be removed from all of Google's domains? Or would his unwilling rise to fame preempt his ability to do so? One could easily argue that Raza's story is of public interest for a variety of reasons, including the fact that the *Star Wars Kid* is frequently cited as the first example of a widely circulated internet meme. One might say that online evidence of Raza's story should not be erased because the evidence itself is an important part of internet history. Indeed, mentions of his story throughout this book appear to support such a conclusion. This leads to another question: How might one assess a similar request from an adult who had intentionally cultivated online fame as an adolescent? Unlike Raza, Christian Akridge, known to his online fans as Christian Leave, put considerable effort into building up his online celebrity and fan base. He has not been a victim but rather has benefited, financially and otherwise, from his social media celebrity. If in another five or fifteen years he grows to regret his adolescent brush with fame, should he be permitted to retroactively erase traces of his earlier online life?

These hypothetical examples suggest that for victims of online notoriety, and even for self-fashioned social media celebrities, the distinction between private citizen and public figure may not prove to be a particularly useful basis upon which to determine who should or should not be able to benefit from data erasure laws. First, social media platforms make it difficult to determine who is a public figure. As the examples of Akridge and countless other social media celebrities (both young and old) demonstrate, it is now possible to become a public figure without an agent and even without leaving one's home. One can gain public celebrity from a private setting, even one's bedroom. While some earlier media phenomena (e.g., reality television) also eroded the boundary between public and private, social media do this in a far more pervasive way, and young people are more widely implicated.[6] A second and equally important consideration is the extent to which online environments merge the experience of being in public with the act of publicity. "There is a big difference between being *in* public and *being* public," observes danah boyd. "Teens want to gather in public environments to socialize, but they do not necessarily want every vocalized expression to be publicized. Yet, because being in a networked public—unlike gathering with friends in a public park—often makes interactions more visible . . . mere participation in social media can blur these two dynamics."[7] While adults are also affected by the blurring of the boundary between private citizens and public figures, the problem is more acute for children and teens.

In the digital world, young people are more likely than ever before to become public figures. Their activities are also more likely to become matters of public interest. For the first time in history, they have access to the technologies required to produce and circulate representations of their lives. But what has not changed is their social and economic status. Children and teens under eighteen are still unable to vote, are unable to make decisions about their own schooling and medical care, and are subject to curfews and other types of physical restrictions. Although they have gained unprecedented access to the tools needed to document and broadcast their lives 24 / 7, their lives are still very much confined to the private sphere and sanctioned institutional settings, such as schools. Their lives can be very public, yet they lack many of the basic rights and freedoms afforded to adults.[8]

Even if there were a societal agreement that digital footprints left by the young should be easier to clean up than those left by adults, and we could easily distinguish between public figures and private citizens, the pace of social media would likely hinder such efforts. Here, it is useful to return to the case of Rehtaeh Parsons.

Parsons's life was destroyed when a compromising photograph of her was taken at a teen party and then put into circulation online. While her suicide was arguably also the result of a marred investigation, the speed at which the compromising photograph circulated was a significant factor. Had the photograph been a Polaroid rather than a digital image, it would never have spread as widely or as quickly. In this case, it is clear how the speed of social media works against the very idea of a moratorium on consequences. After all, the moratorium that Eric Erikson had in mind depends on present events being forgotten and not carried forward into the future.

Ultimately, Parsons's case reminds us that, compared to analogue media, digital media are both unforgiving and "unforgetting." With analogue media, there is invariably a time lag between the moment of production and the moment of broadcasting; in the case of digital media, production and broadcasting often happen simultaneously or nearly simultaneously. Adolescents are in effect no longer documenting their social lives to produce memory objects they can access in the future, but rather experiencing the social world via a documentary platform. Online, social interactions and the documentation of these interactions merge, but this also creates new risks for youth. Unlike the park, the backseat of a car, or a suburban rec room, what unfolds online for youth is, in some respects, already part of the public record. Even if we agreed as a society to look the other way, the conditions to do so are, in effect, already severely eroded. Digital space and digital time both work against the very possibility of a psychosocial moratorium for youth.

Beyond the fact that everything now seems stacked against the conditions required for such a moratorium, there is one more factor that cannot be ignored. Tech-driven economies have little to gain from supporting young people's right to forget and be forgotten. Given that children and teens account for roughly a third of the world's internet users, their participation and willingness to generate data, and keep generating it, is now of great economic importance.[9] As such, current efforts to grant children and youth some form of digital disappearance will probably succeed only to the extent that the desire to forget and be forgotten can be captured and commodified.

Data Dispossession

To appreciate why corporate interests are likely to determine the future of digital disappearance and by extension the future of forgetting, we need to locate both disappearance and forgetting in our current technological and economic landscape.

For decades, fears about surveillance have been on the rise. Yet, most of these fears have proven to be unfounded. In the late twentieth century, surveillance was synonymous with visual technologies. People once predicted that in the twenty-first century we would live in a world where cameras were ubiquitous. Today, video cameras are prevalent, but the thousands of hours of video footage recorded each day represent only a small fraction of the data collected about people. It may not be how or how often we are seen that poses the greatest threat to our privacy, but rather the data we cannot see at all and often do not even know exists.

The most valuable assets held by technology companies are their storehouses of data. Like wood and iron in the nineteenth century, data is now an essential resource. This is why a digital platform that has yet to be monetized can be worth millions, and in the case of Instagram, even a billion dollars.[10] While advertising is certainly a source of immediate revenue, the value of these companies is typically based on their ability to generate data and to use it to produce more data, as well as products or patents. The media theorist Jodi Dean describes this phenomenon as "communicative capitalism." Dean argues that under communicative capitalism, which is now the dominant economic structure across the developed world, the only thing that truly matters is circulation. The specific content of any contribution is secondary to circulation itself. In other words, what messages are being sent, by whom and when, and whether they are ever heard or answered, are irrelevant. As long as data is being generated, the current economic system will continue to thrive.[11]

Here, it is helpful to draw a comparison. Consider the adoption of social media by activists, such as those who gathered together both online and in person in movements such as the Arab Spring, the Occupy movement, and Black Lives Matter. In the past, activists also relied on technologies produced by companies that might not have shared their political goals. For example, Xerox's development of xerographic technologies in the mid-twentieth century was meant to facilitate specific types of office work; but xerography turned out to be an unintended gift to several generations of activists, who relied on it to produce inexpensive posters and pamphlets. While executives and researchers at Xerox and other copy machine manufacturers may not have been entirely oblivious to the subversive ways in which their office machines were being used, they ultimately had no idea exactly what was being copied on their machines. Moreover, because activists often reproduced their materials on copy machines belonging to their employers, the manufacturers also did not directly benefit. As a result, there were few possibilities for these manufacturers to recuperate anything from activists' use of their machines. Today, when activists use platforms such as Facebook, Twitter, and Instagram, those companies can recuperate a great deal. Every tweet, every Facebook update, and every image posted on Instagram generates data that can in turn be put to work for purposes that have nothing to do with the content of these original messages, images, and videos. This is the power of communicative capitalism, which, in Dean's words, "subsumes everything we do" and "turns not just our mediated interactions but all our interactions into raw material for capital."[12] Our data are being "dispossessed."

Capitalism has long rested on accumulation via dispossession. This form of accumulation happens, for example, when a private enterprise encourages workers to pay into a pension fund but then raids the fund and leaves employees empty-handed.[13] Data dispossession extends the logic of late capitalism, but in this case something else is being raided—namely, data; and this now includes the data we generate through our ongoing social interactions. Sometimes data dispossession is obvious—for example, when we have to renew our passwords or update our credit card information for an online store—but it often takes less obvious forms. Data dispossession is also taking place when companies collect, combine, and mine different datasets (e.g., datasets about what types of products we purchase on what days of the week and how often we search our own medical symptoms) to produce new products and services that can be sold back to us. Because small amounts of data rarely hold much value, data dispossession is also a collective experience. What is up for grabs, however, is our mode of being together. Our interactions with each other are being mined for the benefit of private companies.[14] We will have to overcome this new form of dispossession if we want to have any hope of preserving the ability to forget and be forgotten in the future.

The Business of Remembering

Forgetting and being forgotten are not the same thing, but they are closely connected. Forgetting is most often conceived of as a neurological or psychological process. Our brains allow some information to become inaccessible (e.g., information that is no longer relevant) so we can focus on more current and relevant information.[15] Being forgotten is a different story. After all, it is a process that rests entirely on other people's shoulders. But sometimes our own ability to forget is interrupted by other people's failure to forget. If we run into an old friend on the street who brings up a specific person or a shared experience that we have forgotten (perhaps because it was something we had no need to remember, or something negative that we wished to forget), our own forgetting is in turn interrupted. That is, you can be forgotten without forgetting, but achieving forgetting without being forgotten is much more difficult. Being forgotten is ultimately social. This is why social media poses such a threat to the future of forgetting and being forgotten.

If, as Dean argues, we now live in a world where our social relations serve the private benefit of another—where social interactions are "analyzed for past patterns and held for future ones in the interest of squeezing out some competitive advantage"—being forgotten is bound to be viewed as a problem.[16] As private interests become invested in our social relations, forgetting about each other is no longer entirely in our control. Consider, for example, the deep investment a platform like Facebook has in ensuring that we neither forget nor are forgotten by others, even by those others to whom we have not spoken in decades.

When I first signed up for Facebook (not until 2008, and only because I had recently moved to a new country), my intention was to stay connected to people I already knew and had contact with on a regular basis. Initially, my contacts were friends I had just left behind, along with a few new colleagues. As time passed, however, a growing number of acquaintances from the past started to "friend" me. These were people like my old acquaintance Mike, whom I first met at a drama festival in high school. After the weekend festival, Mike and I fell out of touch since he lived a three-hour car ride away, and in the mid-1980s, few teens attempted to maintain relationships across such great distances. Five years later, however, he transferred to my university, and we finally became friends. After graduation we again lost touch—that is, until Facebook came along. When Mike friended me on Facebook nearly fifteen years later, I wondered why. We had not talked to each other in over a decade, and by then, we had nothing but the past in common. Of course, nearly everyone on Facebook has a Mike or a dozen Mikes. These are people with whom we don't mind reconnecting, but they are also people we would likely never think about again had Facebook not created a structure to put us back in touch—because it is invested in our renewed and ongoing communication.

When I eventually chose to deactivate my Facebook account in 2011, another odd thing happened. As I was doing so, I was asked to look at pictures of all the people I might miss if I took this bold step. Mike's face was one of the faces that flashed up on my screen, but so did the faces and names of dozens of people I did not know at all. By then, I had close to seven hundred "friends"—mostly people I had met in passing at conferences or literary events, or people I had never met but with whom I had some sort of professional connection—and while I had no reason to remember these people, it was clear to me that Facebook did. However, the reason why the platform, which has brought millions of old friends and distant relatives and even strangers together, is invested in keeping our relationships alive has very little to do with sentiment. Facebook is invested in everyone remembering and not forgetting for a simple reason. When my old friend Mike shares photos of his kids with me and I "like" them, and when Mike "likes" my posting about a forthcoming book and forwards the link to five other old mutual friends, we are generating data and fostering more connections, which is good for Facebook. If all the Kates and Mikes in the world had chosen forgetting over remembering, Facebook would not be the company it is today.

Today, Facebook is losing popularity among teenagers and young adults, many of whom have described it to me as "social media for old people." They generally prefer Instagram and Snapchat. All three platforms, however, are driven by a similar set of goals. While Facebook wants me to "like" my old friend's pictures of his babies, Instagram and Snapchat have developed other ways to ensure that users are constantly generating more data. Snapchat, for example, introduced a feature called "snapstreaks" in 2016. A snapstreak is achieved when you send direct snaps back and forth to a friend for at least three days. If you and another snapper accomplish this task, an emoji resembling a flame appears next to your names confirming that you are on a streak. A number appears next to the flame emoji to remind you of how many days your streak has lasted. If an hourglass emoji appears, it is a grim reminder that your snapstreak is about to end.[17] While this may sound frivolous, for teens, pressure to keep a streak active can be intense. The journalist Mary Choi, who embedded herself in the social media world of five teenage girls, reported on their use of Snapchat: "The teens I talk to have anywhere from two to 12 streaks going at the same time. They all say it feels a bit like a chore but that it is the perfect level of communication with someone you might not feel close enough to for texting. Most of the dispatches are unflattering images of close-up faces that require about as much effort as an emoji but feel infinitely less generic. . . . Snaps are to let someone know you're thinking of them but perhaps not that hard."[18] Yet, some teens are considerably more invested in snapstreaks. While I was writing this book, I asked several tweens, teens, and college-age young adults why they maintained their snapstreaks. Some said that it was simply an easy way to stay in touch with friends and acquaintances, including those with whom they might not want to have an actual conversation, but others described their snapstreaks as "visible traces" or "evidence" of their friendships and romantic relationships. Snapstreaks evidently feed into teens' strong desire to be in contact with peers on a constant basis but also, and perhaps more importantly, they support the required "ongoingness" of any successful form of communicative capitalism.

The Cost of Forgetting

Forgetting now comes at a huge cost—not to the individuals who once owned their own memories, but rather to a growing range of private entities that are invested in our memories and, by extension, in our collective refusal of forgetting. So, what is the future of forgetting in a world where forgetting now holds great economic consequences? What price will today's children and young adults ultimately pay?

What Problem?

Over the course of working on this book, I had several opportunities to present my work in progress. Wherever I did so, at least one audience member would ask, "Won't we just adapt? Won't these problems be resolved by a modification of expectations and behaviors over time?" I often encountered a strong sense of optimism about the future—a virtually utopian expectation that we will become less preoccupied with other people's digital footprints and more judicious about what we put online in the first place.

This may be true. In the past year or two, a number of high-profile data breaches and scandals concerning release of private data have caused some people to reduce their use of social media. Following the revelation that Facebook had allowed the consulting firm Cambridge Analytica access to over 80 million users' data, for example, thousands of users chose to delete their Facebook accounts.[19] Whether all those users will permanently stay off the platform, and whether such protests will lead to a broader shift in how people engage online, however, is yet to be seen. It is possible that consumer skepticism combined with wide-scale media literacy may mitigate some of the effects of living in a world where data accumulates at a much more rapid pace than in the past. But I have a difficult time believing in the "alternative futures" hypothesis I continue to encounter. This optimistic view entirely ignores the fact that private companies are increasingly invested in our private lives and in the data we generate. To retain at least some form of forgetting, forgetting itself will likely need to become captured, monetized, and used to generate data.

Pay for Delete

One way that deleting data could be monetized would be through a "pay-for-delete" model similar to the system used by some debt collection agencies. In the pay-for-delete system, a debt collector agrees to remove a debt from an individual's credit report in exchange for a payment, usually payment in full. Even though most credit bureaus frown upon these arrangements, collection agencies are empowered to delete collection accounts from reports when they receive payment. Pay for delete can also be done with the original creditors, but unlike collection agencies, these creditors have little motivation to engage in the practice. Most collection agencies purchase debt at a discount (e.g., if you owe $325 to your mobile phone carrier, an agency might purchase the debt for a mere $225 and bet on making money by retrieving the debt in full). The fewer resources an agency spends harassing you to pay off your debt, the higher their rate of return on investment, providing an incentive to make pay-for-delete offers.[20]

Such a system could potentially be set up in other areas of life where one could be negatively affected by certain types of information remaining in circulation. Young people's digital history, for example, can hurt their chances of being admitted to college or getting a job. While maintaining a high GPA, acing one's entrance exams, and developing a strong portfolio of extracurricular activities was once enough to gain entry to a desirable school, in the digital age, high school seniors now face another obstacle—their digital history. Two recent studies found that around one-third of college admissions officers searched applicants online, and up to two-thirds checked their Facebook pages. Thirty to 40 percent reported finding material that left a negative impression.[21] In 2017, an incident at Harvard University reminded college applicants of the profound effect their digital reputation could have. In this highly publicized case, Harvard rescinded offers to ten high school students after they contributed offensive memes to a private Facebook group for accepted students.[22]

Many adolescents do recognize that college admissions officers and future employers are watching. In response, these young people are "packaging, editing, and curating their online identity portrayals."[23] For those who need help, a growing number of college admissions consultants are now adding services with names such as "virtual footprint management" and "virtual footprint check and clean up" to their list of available offerings. These services are rarely able to delete unwanted digital detritus, however. Instead, they help applicants create high-traffic sites—for example, carefully curated LinkedIn pages—that tend to rank high in online searches. In the future, however, it is possible that a new class of brokers will appear to help negotiate deletions—similar to the pay-for-delete option for credit history—to sanitize young people's digital reputations. Parents with the means to purchase such services and their children will benefit. For those who cannot afford such services, it will likely create yet another obstacle to overcome on the pathway to higher education.

Deletion via Data Exchange

Social media platforms have often been hailed as democratizing on the grounds that they are free. Of course, we can only regard them as "free" if we overlook their ability to engage all of us in unpaid data-generating activities. Communicative capitalism captures value from things that were once intangible, including our nostalgia (e.g., through genealogical sites, such as Ancestry.com) and romance (e.g., through dating sites, such as OkCupid). But if this is the case, why can't this new economy also capture value from our desire to forget and be forgotten?

In some respects, attempts to do so already exist. As anyone who has deactivated their Facebook account, or any other social media account, already knows, to complete the process, you must first respond to a survey. As a result, the deactivation process itself generates important data that can be put to work to improve the platform you are abandoning. But this is a one-time occurrence. Could the ability to deactivate or delete certain bits and pieces of data become an ongoing process that continues to capture value over time? This is by no means an unimaginable future scenario.

Part of the "ongoingness" of our data dispossession, as Jodi Dean points out, can be found in the constant demands to update our personal information (e.g., by approving changes to Apple's privacy policy or by constantly updating our passwords). On the surface, these demands are for our own benefit (to provide us with information, or to make our accounts more secure), but they are simultaneously data-generating moments. One can easily imagine a scenario, then, where certain types of digital disappearance—for example, deactivating a social media account or erasing a comment left on a website—might hold for only a set period, after which one would have to renew the request. Such a system would entail some trade-offs. If a high school student desperately wanted to have a photograph permanently deleted from a specific platform because it might harm their college admissions prospects, under this scenario the student could request a deletion but, in exchange, they would have to provide other types of personal data—a process that could in theory be indefinite. Rather than a pay-for-delete scenario, in which one pays a third party to delete or at least manage one's digital footprint (e.g., by creating high-traffic websites that move incriminating information farther down in any search), the data subject would be able to obtain digital deletion through an ongoing data exchange. For example, one might agree to permanently share certain data about themselves (e.g., GPS data from a mobile phone) with a broker, who would agree to pay a domain owner or another entity to delete incriminating information, such as an embarrassing photograph or mention in an online post. The broker could theoretically offer the domain owner a few hundred or a few thousand dollars to delete the image or mention in question, and the data subject would pay the broker back by sharing their personal GPS data not just once but for years thereafter, or even over the course of their lifetime. The broker would benefit by being able to sell the data (and the data of thousands of other similar clients) to companies who collect, combine, and mine data to develop new products or services.

Digital Abstinence

A final potential solution to the problem of the persistent digital footprint is digital abstinence.[24] In theory, a person could choose to have no social media presence at all and therefore generate no digital profile. Unfortunately, this rather obvious solution is also inherently flawed. On the one hand, the digital footprint an adolescent creates while growing up can negatively affect their college and job prospects. On the other hand, because everyone from college admissions counselors to future employers are looking at—and in many cases looking for—their digital footprint, simply opting out is not an answer. In a world where having an online presence is highly valued and is often used as a way to verify claims made in other contexts, such as interviews, pursuing digital abstinence would come at a high price. Having no digital footprint might even be as damaging as having a footprint that painted an unflattering picture. Simply put, complete digital abstinence is not a viable solution.

Over the course of more than two decades of research on the impacts of digital media platforms, I have come to appreciate the fact that whenever a new platform is introduced, fears about its impact on young people inevitably arise. I have also realized that the actual effects are often surprisingly different from what people have predicted. In the mid-1990s, when the internet was first arriving in many family homes, Henry Jenkins reminded educators, parents, and policymakers that "we cannot teach children how to engage in critical thought by denying them access to challenging information and provocative images."[25] The same holds true today. Restricting children's access to new media platforms is unlikely to benefit either children or adults.

Rather than cast digital forgetting as a child or adolescent problem, I suggest that we cast it as a broader societal problem that happens to affect the young in unique and profound ways. Young people will be especially affected by the decline of forgetting not because they are *consumers* of digital media, but rather because they are *producers* of digital media. Earlier panics about new media, such as cinema and television, focused on the fact that children were passive recipients of the messages conveyed by these media. This was never entirely true, and it is certainly not true today. Children and adolescents have a lot at stake in current discussions on forgetting precisely because they play a key role in the contemporary digital economy as both consumers and producers. But unlike adult media producers, children are still marginalized in at least one notable way: they cannot open a Google AdSense account and make money from their visitors' views and clicks.[26] Young people have become fully engaged media producers, but with a few exceptions, they still do not own the means of production. They are integral to the generation of data, which is precisely what drives the digital economy. The value of many companies, especially social media platforms such as Snapchat and Instagram, rests largely on the free digital labor of users, many of whom are minors. But the ability of these young people to directly benefit from the digital economy is severely restricted on the basis of their age alone.

Conclusion

Forgetting, Freedom, and Data

U ntil recently, it was possible to distance ourselves from the most embarrassing and painful parts of our childhood and adolescence. Even twentieth-century personal media devices, from Polaroid cameras to video camcorders, did little to threaten our ability to carry forward only selected memories of our youth. Photographs fade, formats fall into obsolescence, and most forms of analogue media can be erased or destroyed. Now, two decades into the age of digital media, the ability to leave our childhood and adolescent years behind, and to have others forget our younger self, are deeply imperiled—but not because we have lost our desire to sometimes be forgotten by others.

A combination of technological and economic changes has put forgetting and being forgotten at risk for everyone. For young people, there have also been a series of high-stakes tradeoffs. Children and adolescents have finally achieved something previously unobtainable: the ability to represent their own lives from their own perspectives and to share these representations with family and friends, or with millions of strangers. In no other historical period have young people had as much power to self-represent and distribute information. But this freedom has come at a cost, which is only now beginning to become fully apparent.

Until recently, children and adolescents lacked widespread access to image-making and broadcasting technologies because these technologies were either too expensive to purchase or too difficult to use. Moreover, even if a child or teen could afford a Brownie or Polaroid camera and was able to become an expert photographer, developing, duplication, and distribution costs remained prohibitive. To make media technologies and distribution channels widely accessible, even to children and teens, the entire economic structure of media production had to change. This is precisely what has happened since the late 1990s.

Up until this time, technology companies generated revenue primarily by developing and selling hardware (e.g., cameras) and services (e.g., film processing) or, in the case of computers, by selling hardware and software products. Today, more companies are generating revenue either partially or solely from harvesting the data that users produce simply by being online.[1] While most children and teens lack the resources to regularly purchase new cellphones or other expensive hardware, they do have two things that many adults do not, both of which are resources that technology companies are eager to exploit: time, and a burning desire to be constantly in contact with their peers.

It is natural for adolescents to search for a role in society, a search that causes them to form deep bonds with their social cohort.[2] Substantial evidence suggests that adolescents have a very strong need for social identification and validation. We now live in an era when this desire for connectivity and constant validation can be captured and commodified. This desire, which once prompted teens to talk on the phone for hours or to hang out at the mall with their friends, now prompts teens to connect online and, consequently, to engage in data-generating activities. This means that technology companies have good reason to put an entire range of communication technologies in young people's hands and to ensure that they use these technologies as often as possible. "The more active users are," notes the journalist Nancy Jo Sales, "the more data about them social media companies can collect, and the higher they are valued, as they can sell the data to other companies."[3]

While children and teens have benefited from their newfound ability to express themselves, they are already paying and will continue to pay for the control they have gained over the tools needed to self-represent and broadcast texts and images of their own making. These losses are both social and psychological, and they may eventually take other forms.

First, as more young people's lives take place in virtual spaces (and as more events that happen in person are simultaneously recorded and recirculated online), the ability to take normal adolescent risks faces new obstacles. Stupid or embarrassing moments, which are simply part of growing up, hold consequences they did not hold in the past. The psychosocial moratorium—that once granted at least some adolescents a temporary pass on suffering the consequences of their actions—has eroded.

Young people are not only losing some of their ability to explore and try on new identities without consequence. As more of their early years are recorded, they are also losing the ability to edit and curate their childhood memories. Childhood memories, according

to Freud, are not true memories, but rather "screen memories"—
elaborations of memories that have been modified by our later life
experiences. As we move into an era when our childhood memories
will increasingly be "fact-checked," so to speak, by an ever-expanding
mass of searchable data, will these screen memories survive? Is this
yet another intangible price that we will pay for gaining greater
access to the media technologies that allow us to make and distribute images? If so, some children and teens will have much more
to lose than others, especially those who wish to forget traumas or
shameful incidents from their past.

The third tradeoff concerns mobility: the ability to take flight,
leave home, and move on. In the past, if a person outgrew their social
network, they could simply stop responding to phone calls and cut off
contact from people in this network. In the early twenty-first century,
removing oneself from a social network is no longer such a simple
task. In a sense, we now carry our social networks with us wherever
we go. In addition, information that once resided in photo albums and
junk drawers is now networked and tagged. In the past, if you destroyed a photograph, chances are you would never see it again, even
if an old friend happened to have a duplicate in their drawer. Today,
old images in other people's possession, such as scans of high school
yearbook pages, can find us in the present whether we welcome these
intrusions from the past or not. Whether we choose to stay or leave
home, and whether we choose to stay in touch with people from the
past or cut them off, the past can now more easily seep into the present. Neither space nor time serves as a significant barrier.

Although the tradeoffs described here will affect everyone,
children and adolescents have more to lose than adults. In addition,
young people are less well equipped than adults to manage and fight
for their right to be forgotten and the related right to forget. If, as

speculated in Chapter 5, a system develops in which the ability to digitally disappear requires some sort of direct exchange of money, youth, who are already economically marginal, will be less able to access it. They will need to rely on their parents' good will and good judgment to help fund these requests for erasure. It is also possible, however, that parents might pay to have certain aspects of their child's online identity deleted against their child's wishes. Parents might pay to have a child's posts about their sexual preference deleted, for example. If digital disappearance takes a different form, and we have to provide more data to secure the deletion of existing and unwanted data, young people might also have more to lose than adults. They might find themselves caught in an endless loop, experiencing pressure to share and generate data to manage their already unwieldy digital footprints and shadows. The younger a person is when they enter into such an arrangement, the more complex and unwieldy it will be to manage their data subject.

Forgetting, as we have seen throughout this book, is not an entirely negative phenomenon; indeed, it is sometimes a necessity. Despite its bad reputation, forgetting has a function. Forgetting can help one take risks, explore new identities, embrace new ideas; it can help one grow up. Forgetting can function as a convenient crutch to overcome a minor brush with shame or as a panacea for a more severe trauma. Forgetting and being forgotten by others are in this sense synonymous with freedom. To not be tethered to the past by one's own memories—or worse yet, reminders from someone else's memories—is to have the freedom to reimagine oneself in the present and the future. It is precisely because forgetting and freedom are linked that the end of forgetting is of such great consequence, above all for young people.

NOTES

Introduction

1. A 2016 study by Google, summarized on the company's blog on the first anniversary of the release of Google Photos, reported that Google Photo's 200 million users uploaded 24 billion selfies in the previous twelve-month period (https://www.blog.google/products/photos/google-photos-one-year-200 -million/). Finding accurate data on the number of selfies taken by age group, however, is more challenging. At least one study found that younger people, especially young women, take and circulate more selfies. See the SelfieCity investigation, a large-scale project that gathered data on the number and type of selfies taken in five major cities around the world: http://selfiecity.net.

2. Danielle Wiener-Browner, "Narcissistic Babies Can't Stop Taking Selfies," *Atlantic*, Jan. 28, 2014.

3. John Schwartz, "Caution: Children at Play on the Information Highway," *Washington Post*, Nov. 28, 1993, A01.

4. See U.S. Department of Health and Human Services, *Physical Activity and Health: A Report of Health of the Surgeon General* (Atlanta: U.S. Department of Health and Human Services, Centers for Disease Control and Prevention, National Center for Chronic Disease Prevention and Health Promotion, 1996); J. O. Hill and J. C. Peter, "Environmental Contributions to the Obesity Epidemic," *Science* 280 (1998): 1371–1374; R. Kraut, M. Patterson, V. Lundmark, et al.,

"Internet Paradox: A Social Technology That Reduces Social Involvement and Psychological Well-being?" *American Psychologist* 53 (1998): 1017–1031; Kaveri Subrahmanyam, Robert E. Kraut, Patricia M. Greenfield, and Elisheva F. Gross, "The Impact of Home Computer Use on Children's Activities and Development," *Children and Computer Technology* 10, no. 2 (2000): 123–144.

5. Schwartz, "Caution."

6. Telecommunications Act of 1996, S.652, 104th Cong. (1996).

7. Henry Jenkins, "Empowering Children in the Digital Age: Towards a Radical Media Pedagogy," *Radical Teacher* no. 50 (Spring 1997): 30–35.

8. Neil Postman, *The Disappearance of Childhood* (New York: Delacorte Press, 1982), 85.

9. Other scholars had made the same point. Philippe Ariès argued that after the invention of movable type, children were effectively removed from the adult world to which they had once had access and were then put into schools, where their agency was further stripped away. Ariès, *Centuries of Childhood: A Social History of Family Life*, trans. Robert Baldick (New York: Vintage, 1962), 413. Elizabeth Eisenstein, building on this claim, wrote: "Insofar as printing led to new forms of cumulative cognitive advance and incremental change, it also widened the gap between literate and oral cultures in a manner that placed the well-read adult at an increasing distance from the unschooled small child." Eisenstein, *The Printing Press as an Agent of Change: Communications and Cultural Transformations in Early Modern Europe* (Cambridge: Cambridge University Press, 1979), 432.

10. Ariès, *Centuries of Childhood*, 150–151; Teresa Michals, *Books for Children, Books for Adults: Age and the Novel from Defoe to James* (Cambridge: Cambridge University Press, 2014), 36.

11. Postman, *The Disappearance of Childhood*, 80.

12. Ibid., 149–150.

13. The historian Marianne Hirsch associates such longing with the "postgeneration"—children of Holocaust survivors, whose childhoods were structured by the aporias that so often accompany posttraumatic stress. Hirsch, "The Generation of Postmemory," *Poetics Today* 29, no. 1 (2008): 103–128.

14. In "The Generation of Postmemory," Hirsch argues that photography played a profound role in the experience of the postgeneration. She suggests that the

technology of photography, which promises to offer access to events one never witnessed firsthand, served as a bridge between the Holocaust generation and the generation that followed.

15. Julia Creet, "The Archive as Temporary Abode," in *Memory and Migration: Multidisciplinary Approaches to Memory Studies,* ed. Julia Creet and Andreas Kitzmann (Toronto: University of Toronto Press, 2011), 280–298.

16. Since the 1980s, Germans and, to a lesser extent, people of German heritage around the world have turned their attention to grappling with their parents' and grandparents' connections to the Nazi Party. Some Germans use *Familien-aufstellung,* a form of group therapy, to come to terms their family's complicity in the Holocaust. Burkhard Bilger, "Where Germans Make Peace with Their Dead," *New Yorker,* Sept. 12, 2017.

17. See Hirsh, "The Generation of Postmemory."

18. In this book, "memory studies" refers to the relatively recent field that has arisen in the social sciences and humanities since the 1990s. This field is largely concerned with collective memory rather than individual memory, which is the primary focus of the more established field of experimental memory studies based in the applied sciences. Memory studies in the social sciences and humanities incorporates a specific ethics and politics. In the inaugural issue of *Memory Studies* in 2008, Susannah Radstone emphasizes that memory research "goes to the heart of many of the issues at the forefront of contemporary political debate and struggle" to the extent that it is concerned with the continuing presence of the past in the present. Radstone, "Memory Studies: For and Against," *Memory Studies* 1, no. 1 (2008): 31–39.

19. For an overview of this work, see Jeffrey K. Olick, *The Sins of the Fathers: Germany, Memory, Method* (Chicago: University of Chicago Press, 2016).

20. Paul Ricoeur, *Memory, History, Forgetting,* trans. Kathleen Blamey and David Pellauer (Chicago: University of Chicago Press, 2004), 413.

21. I should point out that while forgetting carries a mostly negative connotation in memory studies in the social sciences and humanities (because of the field's focus on collective traumas and reparative acts), it is often viewed in a positive light in experimental psychology. For views of forgetting as a necessary and beneficial function, see Benjamin C. Storm, "The Benefit of Forgetting in Thinking and Remembering," *Current Directions in Psychological Science* 20,

no. 5 (2011): 291–295; Michael C. Anderson and Simon Hanslmayr, "Neural Mechanisms of Motivated Forgetting," *Trends in Cognitive Psychology* 18, no. 6 (2014): 279–292; Blake A. Richards and Paul W. Frankland, "The Persistence and Transciences of Memory," *Neuron* 94, no. 6 (2017): 1071–1084.

22. Shoshana Felman and Dori Laub, *Testimony: Crises of Witnessing in Literature, Psychoanalysis, and History* (New York: Routledge, 1992), 67.

23. Ibid., 122–123.

24. Matthew Brunwasser, "A 21st-Century Migrant's Essentials: Food, Shelter, Smartphone," *New York Times,* Aug. 25, 2015, A1.

25. A series in the *New York Times* in 2016 featuring stories about Canada's new Syrian arrivals profiled one couple that was so tethered to their past lives that they were at times unable to sleep or carry out basic tasks—not due to their trauma but rather due to the digital presence of the people they were forced to leave behind. Jodi Kantor and Catrin Einhorn, "What Does It Mean to Help One Family?" *New York Times,* Sept. 8, 2016.

26. Barbie Zelizer, *Remembering to Forget: Holocaust Memory through the Camera's Eye* (Chicago: University of Chicago Press, 1998).

27. Maggie Schauer, Frank Neuner, and Thomas Elbert, *Narrative Exposure Therapy: A Short-Term Treatment for Traumatic Stress Disorders,* 2nd ed. (Cambridge, MA: Hogrefe Publishing, 2011).

28. Sigmund Freud, "Remembering, Repeating and Working-Through," in *The Standard Edition of the Complete Psychological Works of Sigmund Freud,* vol. 12, ed. J. Strachey (London: Hogarth Press, 1994), 151.

29. Jorge Luis Borges, "Funes the Memorious," in *Labyrinths: Selected Stories and Other Writings* (New York: New Directions, 1964), 63–64.

30. Sigmund Freud, "Childhood and Concealing Memories," in *Psychopathology of Everyday Life,* trans. A. A. Brill (New York: Macmillan, 1915), 63.

31. Despite the widespread acceptance of Freud's theories in some disciplines, his concept of repression is still not universally accepted. In a 2006 article on repression, Matthew Erdelyi remarks that scientific psychologists are unsure whether repression is "an obvious fact of mental life or an outright (and even dangerous) myth." Erdelyi himself contends that repression is a fact, noting that both laboratory and clinical studies have found evidence that people omit some memories while elaborating on others and do so for a range of reasons. Matthew

Hugh Erdelyi, "The Unified Theory of Repression," *Behavioral and Brain Science* 29, no. 5 (2006): 499–511. Two articles critiquing Erdelyi's work appeared in the same issue of the journal; see Simon Boag, "Can Repression Become a Conscious Process?" and Harlene Hayne, Maryanne Garry, and Elizabeth F. Loftus, "On the Continuing Lack of Scientific Evidence for Repression," *Behavioral and Brain Science* 29, no. 5 (2006): 513–514, and 521–522. For a more extended argument against the concept of repression, see Lawrence Patihis, Scott O. Lilienfeld, Lavina Y. Ho, and Elizabeth F. Loftus, "Unconscious Repressed Memory Is Scientifically Questionable," *Psychological Science*, 25, no. 10 (2014): 1967–1968.

32. Donna J. Bridge and Joel L. Voss, "Hippocampal Binding of Novel Information with Dominant Memory Traces Can Support Both Memory Stability and Change," *Journal of Neuroscience* 34 no. 6 (2014): 2203–2213.

33. Freud, "Childhood and Concealing Memories," 64.

34. There is growing evidence that childhood amnesia occurs in all demographic groups. A 2005 study, for example, investigated the memories of research subjects between six and nineteen years old. Although six- to nine-year-olds could recall earlier events than ten- to nineteen-year-olds, there were otherwise few differences in the structure, social orientation (e.g., whether the memory was an individual one or one experienced by other participants), or nature of the recalled events. Carole Peterson, Valerie V. Grant, and Lesley D. Boland, "Childhood Amnesia in Children and Adolescents: Their Earliest Memories," *Memory* 13, no. 6 (2005): 622–637.

35. Arnold van Gennep, *The Rites of Passage,* trans. Monika B. Vizedom and Gabrielle L. Caffee (New York: Routledge, 2004), 81.

36. European Commission, Factsheet on the "Right to be Forgotten" Ruling (C-131/12), https://www.inforights.im/media/1186/cl_eu_commission _factsheet_right_to_be-forgotten.pdf. Somewhat surprisingly, there is not much literature on digital forgetting beyond the expansive legal literature that has been published, especially in response to the European Union's General Data Protection Regulation, which includes language to protect citizens' "right to be forgotten." The best comprehensive overview of digital forgetting is Viktor Mayer-Schönberger, *Delete: The Virtue of Forgetting in a Digital Era,* paperback ed. (Princeton: Princeton University Press, 2011).

Chapter One. Documenting Childhood before and after Social Media

1. Philippe Ariès, *Centuries of Childhood: A Social History of Family Life*, trans. Robert Baldick (New York: Vintage, 1962); Jenifer Neils and John H. Oakley, *Coming of Age in Ancient Greece: Images of Childhood from the Classical Past* (Hanover, NH: Hood Museum of Art, 2003).

2. Philippe Ariès noted that it was not until the seventeenth century that family portraits began to center around the child (*Centuries of Childhood*, 46–47).

3. In *Centuries of Childhood*, Ariès claimed that the concept of childhood first emerged in the early sixteenth century. This thesis has been widely critiqued. While many critics have cited Ariès's methodological errors, others have noted that he failed to pay attention to class differences. Lawrence Stone, for example, observed, "Ariès's book is in fact a history of French schools, and of upper-class and middle-class parents and children, that lacks the necessary historical context of time, place, class, and culture. A fascinating pioneering book, it is now recognized to be badly flawed in both its methodology and its conclusions." Stone, "The Massacre of the Innocents," *New York Review of Books*, Nov. 14, 1974.

4. Cecile M. Jagodzinski, *Privacy and Print: Reading and Writing in Seventeenth-Century England* (Charlottesville: University Press of Virginia, 1999), 12.

5. Elizabeth Eisenstein, *The Printing Press as an Agent of Change: Communications and Cultural Transformations in Early Modern Europe* (Cambridge: Cambridge University Press, 1979), 431.

6. Michel Foucault, *Discipline and Punish*, trans. Alan Sheridan (New York: Vintage, 1977), 192.

7. Helmut Gernsheim and Alison Gernsheim, *The History of Photography: From the Camera Obscura to the Beginning of the Modern Era* (New York: McGraw-Hill, 1969), 119, 234.

8. Ibid., 234.

9. Even children who died as infants were frequently photographed. Indeed, postmortem photography of infants and children was a widespread practice in the nineteenth century. See Beth Ann Guynn, "Postmortem Photography," in *Encyclopedia of Nineteenth-Century Photography*, ed. John Hannavy (New York: Routledge, 2008), 1165.

10. *Kodakery, A Magazine for Amateur Photographers* first appeared in 1913; all references in this book refer to the edition published in Toronto by Canadian Kodak, Co., Limited.

11. Todd Gustavson, *Camera: The History of Photography from Daguerreotype to Digital* (New York: Sterling Innovation, 2009), 140 (quotation), 162.

12. Eastman once told his employees, "What we do during our working hours determines what we have in the world. What we do in our play hours determines what we are." The dictum suggests that Eastman not only valued play but may even have viewed it as something that could be turned into a valuable resource. See Elizabeth Brayer, *George Eastman: A Biography* (Rochester, NY: University of Rochester Press, 2006), 346.

13. The Brownie was not simply a successful model of camera but represented an innovative approach to marketing. Early on, Eastman Kodak recognized the value of producing devices in compact sizes and multiple colors. Just like Apple's iPods and iPhones, the compact 1957 Brownie Starflash was issued in a spectrum of colors, including black, red, white, and blue, and in a special Coca-Cola-themed edition. Gustavson, *Camera*, 153.

14. Gustavson, *Camera*, 153.

15. Hazen Trayvor, "'Step-in' Pictures," *Kodakery* 10, no. 8 (June 1923), 5.

16. "The School Bell," *Kodakery* 10, no. 12 (Oct. 1923), 5.

17. Sigmund Freud, "Screen Memories," in *The Standard Edition of the Complete Psychological Works of Sigmund Freud,* vol. 6, ed. J. Strachey (London: Hogarth Press, 1960), 43–52.

18. Gustavson, *Camera*, 142.

19. U.S. Department of Labor, Bureau of Labor Statistics, "Union Scale of Wages and Hours of Labor, 1907 to 1912," *Bulletin of the United Sates Bureau of Labor Statistics* 131, Aug. 15, 1913, https://fraser.stlouisfed.org/files/docs/publications /bls/bls_0131_1913.pdf.

20. Some early children's cameras came with development kits, including the Ensign Mickey Mouse camera (ca. 1935) and the Kookie Kamera by Ideal Toy Corporation (ca. 1968). Gustavson, *Camera*, 162–163.

21. Quoted in Eric Zorn, "Reeling Off America at Its Weirdest," *Chicago Tribune,* Jan. 13, 1986, A1.

22. Monique Mattei Ferraro and Eoghan Casey, *Investigating Child Exploitation and Pornography: The Internet, the Law and Forensic Science* (New York: Elsevier, 2005), 14.

23. Gustavson, *Camera*, 306.

24. Peter Buse, *The Camera Does the Rest: How Polaroid Changed Photography* (Chicago: University of Chicago Press, 2016), 31.

25. Ibid., 31, 34 (quotation).

26. Ibid., 7.

27. In his history of the Polaroid camera, Christopher Bonanos notes that there is evidence that Polaroid cameras were used to document things that might have otherwise been censored, including homoerotic images, images depicting fetish cultures, and child pornography. Bonanos, *Instant: The Story of Polaroid* (New York: Princeton Architectural Press, 2012), 73.

28. Buse, *The Camera Does the Rest,* 69.

29. Ibid., 103.

30. Ibid., 31.

31. Some initiatives, such as the African American Home Movie Archive (http://aahma.org/), have put together centralized databases of home movies with a specific focus. Others, such as the Home Movie Archive at the University of Massachusetts Lowell (http://libguides.uml.edu/UMLHomeMovieArchive), house general collections of home movies.

32. Oliver Stone's 1991 film *JFK* offers one example of how different types of media are used to signal memories and flashbacks in film.

33. Patricia R. Zimmermann, "Introduction," in *Mining the Home Movies: Excavations in Histories and Memories,* ed. Karen L. Ishizuka and Patricia R. Zimmermann (Berkeley: University of California Press, 2008), 22.

34. Patricia R. Zimmermann, *Reel Families: A Social History of Amateur Film* (Bloomington: Indiana University Press, 1995), 153.

35. Frederick T. Hollowell, "'Love by Proxy': The First Amateur Motion Picture Production," *Amateur Movie Makers* 1, no. 1 (Dec. 1926): 16.

36. In 1923, a Ciné Kodak Model A camera cost $125; an entire kit, which included a camera, tripod, splicer, projector, and screen, cost $325. Libby Bischof, "A Region Apart," in *Amateur Movie Making: Aesthetics of the*

is attitude is captured by Howard Rheingold in his introduction to the
al edition of *The Virtual Community: Homesteading on the Electronic
er:* "There is no such thing as a single, monolithic, online subculture; it's
ike an ecosystem of subcultures, some frivolous, others serious. The
g edge of scientific discourse is migrating to virtual communities. . . . At
ne time, activists and educational reformers are using the same medium
litical tool. You can use virtual communities to find a date, sell a
ower, publish a novel, conduct a meeting. Some people use virtual
unities as a form of psychotherapy. Others . . . spend eighty hours a week
e pretending they are someone else, living a life that does not exist
e a computer." Rheingold, *The Virtual Community: Homesteading on the
nic Frontier* (Reading, MA: Addison-Wesley, 1993); available at
www.rheingold.com/vc/book/intro.html.

chapter on this research was originally accepted for publication in a
tion edited by Mary Flanagan and Austin Booth, *ReLoad: Rethinking
n in Cyberspace,* published by MIT Press in 2002. In the end, I withdrew
ay from the collection due to ethical concerns. Those of us who were
sed in studying online communities and practices had at best a tenuous
standing of the identities and communities we were investigating in the
I had many lingering questions about the ethics of writing about these
people's personal websites. Was I writing about texts? If so, were they
or private? Or was I peering into these young people's private spaces?
y research more akin to eavesdropping on conversations in someone's
om without their permission, or to analyzing someone's published and
thoughts? As humorous as these concerns may sound over two decades
hey were pressing questions for many researchers engaged in what was at
ne sometimes simply labeled "internet research." Two decades later these
l concerns about protecting my research subjects also reveal just how
ing privacy questions were in the early years of web-based communities.

erry Turkle, *Life on the Screen: Identity in the Age of the Internet* (New
Simon and Schuster, 1995), 177.

id., 10.

e Rheingold, *The Virtual Community.*

rkle, *Life on the Screen,* 10, 11.

would become increasingly apparent that even early online communities
ot entirely separate from the material world, and Turkle's early work has

Everyday in New England Film, 1915–1960, ed. Martha J. McNamara and Karan Sheldon (Bloomington: University of Indiana Press, 2017), 42.

37. Quoted in Zimmermann, *Reel Families,* 134.

38. Zimmermann, *Reel Families,* 134.

39. Gerald Stanley Lee, "Slow Movies for Quick People," *Amateur Movie Makers* 2, no. 2 (Feb. 1927): 99.

40. Zoe Beloff in conversation with Niels Van Tomme, "Dreamland: The Intimate Politics of Desire," *Art Papers* (July / Aug. 2010): 31.

41. Zimmermann, *Reel Families,* 113.

42. David Buckingham, Rebekah Willett, and Maria Pini, *Home Truths? Video Production and Domestic Life* (Ann Arbor: University of Michigan Press, 2011), 9–10.

43. The media studies scholar Susanna Paasonen contends that video cameras and videocassette recorders transformed domestic porn video production, leading to what she describes as the "first wave of amateur porn." Digital imaging technologies built on this, bringing amateur porn production in new directions in the 1990s and 2000s. Paasonen, *Carnal Resonance: Affect and Online Pornography* (Cambridge, MA: MIT Press, 2011), 72.

44. Steven A. Booth, "Electronics," *Popular Mechanics* (May 1987): 60.

45. Sadie Benning, *Me & Rubyfruit* (1989).

46. Stephen Hayman, "Photos, Photos Everywhere," *New York Times,* July 29, 2015.

47. See Rose Eveleth, "How Many Photographs of You Are Out There in the World?" *Atlantic,* Nov. 2, 2015.

48. This book uses examples almost exclusively from North America and Europe. This partially reflects the fact that digital technologies are not equally accessible across regions. According to a 2017 UNICEF report, 96 percent of youth (fifteen- to twenty-four-year-olds) in Europe were online, compared with only 40 percent in Africa. Overall, children and adolescents under eighteen account for one-third of internet users around the world, and youth are the most connected demographic in the world: 71 percent are online, compared with 48 percent of the total population. United Nations Children's Fund (UNICEF), "Children in a Digital World," The State of the World's Children 2017, "Key

Messages," p. 1, https://www.unicef.org/publications/files/SOWC_2017_ENG _WEB.pdf.

49. See Patricia G. Lange and Mizuko Ito, "Creative Production," in *Hanging Out, Messing Around, and Geeking Out,* ed. Mizuko Ito, Sonja Baumer, Matteo Bittanti, et al. (Cambridge, MA: MIT Press, 2010), 291.

Chapter Two. Forgetting and Being Forgotten in the Age of the Data Subject

1. European Commission, Factsheet on the "Right to be Forgotten" Ruling (C-131/12), https://www.inforights.im/media/1186/cl_eu_commission _factsheet_right_to_be-forgotten.pdf.

2. Viviane Reding, "The EU Data Protection Reform 2012: Making Europe the Standard Setter for Modern Data Protection Rules in the Digital Age," address given at the Innovation Conference Digital, Life, Design, Munich, Jan. 22, 2012, http://europa.eu/rapid/press-release_SPEECH-12-26_en.htm.

3. Article 38 of the European Union's General Data Protection Regulation includes the following statement: "Children merit specific protection with regard to their personal data, as they may be less aware of the risks, consequences and safeguards concerned and their rights in relation to the processing of personal data. Such specific protection should, in particular, apply to the use of personal data of children for the purposes of marketing or creating personality or user profiles and the collection of personal data with regard to children when using services offered directly to a child. The consent of the holder of parental responsibility should not be necessary in the context of preventive or counselling services offered directly to a child." See "Regulation (EU) 2016/679 of the European Parliament and of the Council of 27 April 2016 on the Protection of Natural Persons with Regard to the Processing of Personal Data and on the Free Movement of Such Data, and Repealing Directive 95/46/EC," https://eur-lex.europa.eu/legal-content/EN/TXT/PDF/?uri=CELEX:32016 R0679&from=EN.

4. California Business and Professional Code section 22580, SB-568, Privacy: Internet: minors (2013–2014), http://leginfo.legislature.ca.gov/faces/codes _displaySection.xhtml?lawCode=BPC&sectionNum=22580.

5. Sonia Livingstone, "Children's Privacy Rights Are Prominent in the Data Protection Bill but There's Many a Slip . . . ," Media Policy Project blog post, London School of Economics and Political Science, Aug. 14, 2017, http://blogs

.lse.ac.uk/mediapolicyproject/2017/08/14/childr -prominent-in-the-data-protection-bill-but-there

6. In the late twentieth century in Canada, for e: nation's longstanding residential school system fe a convenient way for the nation not only to distan that occurred in these schools but also to forget al colony of Britain. Similarly, in the United States, have permitted policymakers to avoid addressing continue to promote social and economic disparit forgetting is most often seen as the opposite of co Ben-Yehuda observes that they are "two ends of tl selecting historical facts and events." Ben-Yehuda *Memory and Mythmaking in Israel* (Madison: Uni 1995), 302.

7. Friedrich Nietzsche, *On the Genealogy of Mor* (Cambridge: Cambridge University Press, 2006), 3

8. Frederic C. Bartlett, *Remembering: A Study in Psychology* (London: Cambridge University Press,

9. Michael C. Anderson and Simon Hanslmayr, " Motivated Forgetting," *Trends in Cognitive Scienc*

10. Benjamin C. Storm, "The Benefit of Forgettir membering," *Current Directions in Psychological* 294–295.

11. Antoinette Rouvroy, "Réinventer l'art d'oublier société de l'information?" in *La sécurité de l'indivi prospectives et internationales,* ed. Stéphanie Laco 2008), 249–278, available at https://works.bepress /(translation my own, emphasis in the original).

12. For more information on DeadSocial, a self-de service," visit its homepage: http://deadsocial.org/.

13. For more information on EU General Data Pro nongovernmental information portal, http://www.

14. Bert-Jaap Koops, "Forgetting Footprints, Shur Analysis of the 'Right to Be Forgotten' in Big Data I (2011): 234, 254.

15. T

origin

Front

more

cuttin

the sa

as a p

lawnn

comm

or mo

outsid

Electr

http://

16. A

collec

Wome

my es

imme

under

1990s

young

public

Was m

bedro

public

later,

the ti

ethica

confu

17. S

York:

18. Ib

19. S

20. T

21. It

were

been criticized for reinforcing a false binary between the virtual and the real. At the time of its publication, however, *Life on the Screen* did capture a widely shared perception of emerging virtual spaces and their relationship to the so-called real world.

22. Erik H. Erikson, *Childhood and Society,* 2nd ed. (New York: Norton, 1963), 262–263.

23. Turkle, *Life on the Screen,* 203.

24. While this may be true within many communities, it is important to point out that experimenting and even engaging in "delinquent" behavior comes at a much higher cost to some young people than to others. A white adolescent who steals an item of clothing from a retailer may be caught, but few white adolescent shoplifters face severe penalties for their petty crimes. A black adolescent caught stealing the same item of clothing in the same context is far more likely to be permanently affected by the infraction. According to the NAACP, African American children represent 32 percent of children arrested, 42 percent of children detained, and 52 percent of children whose cases are judicially waived to criminal court. NAACP, Criminal Justice Factsheet, http://www.naacp.org/criminal-justice-fact-sheet.

25. Erik Erikson, *Identity: Youth and Crisis* (New York: Norton, 1968), 157.

26. Turkle, *Life on the Screen,* 203.

27. Ibid., 204.

28. Erikson, *Childhood and Society,* 263.

29. This trend was already firmly established by 2012. At the time, the *Harvard Business Review* ran an article ominously titled, "Your Future Employer Is Watching You Online. You Should Be, Too." The author, Michael Fertik, writes, "Already, recruiters and hiring managers are relying heavily on the internet to research candidates for employment. Multiple studies show convincingly that more than 75% of employers actively research candidates online. They show further that more than 70% have decided NOT to hire a candidate based on what they've found. Recruiters have been shown to not just look people up on search engines, but to dig very deep, through social media profiles, shopping profiles, online gaming sites, classifieds, and auction sites (think eBay and Craigslist)—and even in virtual worlds like SecondLife!" Fertik, "Your Future Employer Is Watching You Online. You Should Be, Too," *Harvard Business Review,* Apr. 3, 2012, https://hbr.org/2012/04/your-future-employer-is-watchi.

30. Natasha Singer, "New Item on College Admission Checklist: LinkedIn Profile," *New York Times,* Nov. 5, 2016, BU6.

31. Viktor Mayer-Schönberger, *Delete: The Virtue of Forgetting in the Digital Age* (Princeton: Princeton University Press, 2009), 172.

32. danah boyd, *It's Complicated: The Social Lives of Networked Teens* (New Haven: Yale University Press, 2014), 64.

33. Since at least 2014, there have been third-party apps such as Snapsaved that help Snapchat users preserve their snaps. While users have generally welcomed such interventions, Snapsaved came under attack. Indeed, it was blamed when an estimated two hundred thousand snaps were hacked in 2014 and allegedly ended up on the dark web. Caitlin Dewey, "The Snappening Is Not a Hoax," *Washington Post,* Oct. 4, 2014.

34. Franziska Roesner, Brian T. Gill, and Tadayoshi Kohno, "Sex, Lies, or Kittens? Investigating the Use of Snapchat's Self-Destructing Messages," in *Financial Cryptography and Data Security,* ed. Sarah Meiklejohn and Kazue Sako (New York: Springer, 2014), 67.

35. boyd, *It's Complicated,* 64.

36. Snapchat's Infinity setting was introduced on May 9, 2017: https://www.snap.com/en-US/news/post/limitless-snaps.

37. Susan Stewart, *On Longing: Narratives on the Miniature, the Gigantic, the Souvenir, the Collection* (Durham, NC: Duke University Press, 1993), 167.

Chapter Three. Screens, Screen Memories, and Childhood Celebrity

1. Anita Gates, "Gary Coleman, 'Diff'rent Strokes' Star, Dies at 42," *New York Times,* May 28, 2010, A23.

2. Associated Press, "Dana Plato, 34, Star of 'Diff'rent Strokes,'" *New York Times,* May 10, 1999; Virginia Heffernan, "Revealing the Wages of Young Sitcom Fame," *New York Times,* Sept. 4, 2006.

3. Todd Bridges with Sarah Tomlinson, *Killing Willis: From Diff'rent Strokes to the Mean Streets to the Life I Always Wanted* (New York: Simon and Schuster, 2011).

4. See the New York State Department of Labor's regulation on child performers (https://labor.ny.gov/workerprotection/laborstandards/secure/child_index.shtm) and the "Coogan Law" (https://www.sagaftra.org

/membership-benefits/young-performers/coogan-law/coogan-law-full-text), which is in effect in only four states: New York, California, Louisiana, and New Mexico.

5. In the states where the Coogan Law is in effect any monetization of a child's social media celebrity should be subject to the law, but there is considerable ambiguity since historically, child entertainers have been considered employed but child and teen social media celebrities are not technically employed. In 2017, a *New York Times* reporter asked a California-based attorney whether the Coogan Law applied to child social media celebrities. His response was, "These are uncharted waters." Katherine Rosman, "Why Isn't Your Toddler Paying the Mortgage?" *New York Times,* Sept. 27, 2017.

6. Ian Austen, "2 Survivors of Canada's First Quintuplet Clan Reluctantly Re-emerge," *Globe and Mail,* Apr. 3, 2017, A1.

7. Sarah J. Schoppe-Sullivan, Jill E. Yavorsky, Mitchell K. Bartholomew, et al., "Doing Gender Online: New Mothers' Psychological Characteristics, Facebook Use, and Depressive Symptoms," *Sex Roles* 76, no. 5–6 (2017): 276.

8. Parent Zone, "Today's Children Will Feature in Almost 1,000 Online Photos by the Time They Reach Age Five," Nominet, May 26, 2015, https://www
.nominet.uk/todays-children-will-feature-in-almost-1000-online-photos-by
-the-time-they-reach-age-five/.

9. Mott Poll Report, "Parents on Social Media: Likes and Dislikes of Sharenting," National Poll on Children's Health, C. S. Mott Children's Hospital, University of Michigan, Mar. 16, 2015, https://mottpoll.org/sites/default/files/documents
/031615_sharenting_0.pdf.

10. Ibid.

11. Jesse Mab-Phea Hill, "Shitty Day," Parenthood: The Struggle blog, https://parenthoodthestruggle.wordpress.com/2017/05/20/shitty-day/.

12. Vine was a video-hosting site founded in 2012. By 2015, the site had an estimated 200 million users. In 2016 it was suddenly shut down, though its content remains accessible. Vine videos were distributed both on Vine and on other social media sites, including Facebook and Twitter.

13. Brian Feldman, "Who Is Gavin? And Why Has He Taken Over Twitter?" *New York Magazine* Intelligencer, Aug. 12, 2016, http://nymag.com/selectall
/2016/08/meet-gavin-the-five-year-old-meme-star.html.

14. Helin Jung, "What It's Really Like to Be a Yelp Celebrity When You're Not Even 2 Years Old," *Cosmopolitan* Cosmo Bites, June 22, 2015, http://www.cosmopolitan.com/food-cocktails/a42238/foodbaby-is-living-the-dream/.

15. Simon Nørby, "Why Forget? On the Adaptive Value of Memory Loss," *Perspectives on Psychological Science* 10, no. 5 (2015): 553, 554.

16. Benoit Denizet-Lewis, "Following Christian Leave: The Strange Life of a Teen Social Media Celebrity," *Rolling Stone*, Dec. 8, 2015, http://www.rollingstone.com/culture/features/can-a-kid-from-texas-survive-the-new-rules-of-teen-celebrity-20151208.

17. PressPlay's featured talent frequently changes, but their roster of talent always includes more young men than young women, with young men typically accounting for 85–100 percent of featured performers at live events. By contrast, images on the PressPlay website reveal that the "fans" are nearly exclusively adolescent girls. PressPlay, http://pressplay.co/talent/.

18. Taylor Lorenz, "Raising a Social-Media Star," *Atlantic,* Jan. 17, 2018.

19. Ibid.

20. The concept of cyberbullying gained currency in the first decade of the twenty-first century after the rise of several high-profile online bullying incidents. Like the term "bullying," which is most often used to describe situations in which children and adolescents are mentally or physically abused by their peers, "cyberbullying" is generally used to describe forms of abuse that are peer-driven, with the difference that the acts of isolation and extortion take place on the internet (e.g., through the circulation of images and videos that are intended to shame the victim). Since 2000, cyberbullying has become increasingly widespread, largely due to the fact that during this period, young people increasingly gained access to their own digital devices. In 2017, about 15 percent of high school students reported experiencing some form of electronic bullying in the previous twelve-month period. Centers for Disease Control and Prevention, "Prevent Bullying" feature, https://www.cdc.gov/features/prevent-bullying/index.html.

21. Although Ghyslain Raza attempted to hide his identity for many years, in his twenties, when he was a law student, he decided to attach his identity to the video once again after having witnessed a rash of cyberbullying incidents leading to suicides. For this reason, his full name is used in this chapter.

22. Amy Harmon, "Compressed Data; Fame Is No Laughing Matter for the 'Star Wars Kid,'" *New York Times,* May 19, 2003.

23. "Star Wars Kid Files Lawsuit," *Wired,* July 24, 2003.

24. Jasmine Garsd, "Internet Memes and 'The Right to Be Forgotten,'" All Tech Considered, NPR, Mar. 3, 2015, http://www.npr.org/sections/alltechconsidered /2015/03/03/390463119/internet-memes-and-the-right-to-be-forgotten.

25. danah boyd, *It's Complicated: The Social Lives of Networked Teens* (New Haven: Yale University Press, 2014), 146.

26. "Ten Years Later, 'Star Wars Kid' Speaks Out," *MacLean's,* May 9, 2013, http://www.macleans.ca/education/uniandcollege/10-years-later-star-wars -kid-speaks-out/.

27. The links between cyberbullying and suicide are now well established. See, for example, Robin M. Kowalski, Gary W. Giumetti, Amber N. Schroeder, and Micah R. Lattanner, "Bullying in the Digital Age: A Critical Review and Meta-Analysis of Cyberbullying Research among Youth," *Psychological Bulletin* 140, no. 4 (2014): 1073–1137; Sameer Hinduja and Justin W. Patchin, "Bullying, Cyberbullying, and Suicide," *Archives of Suicide Research* 14, no. 3 (2010): 206–221; Anat Brunstein Klomek, Frank Marrocco, Marjorie Kleinman, et al., "Peer Victimization, Depression, and Suicidality in Adolescents," *Suicide and Life-Threatening Behavior* 38, no. 2 (2008): 166–180. Gender influences cyberbullying, with young women more likely to find themselves victims of cyberstalking (using electronic communication to stalk another person by sending repeated threatening messages) and unwanted sexting (distributing nude pictures of another individual without that person's consent); see Allyson L. Dir, Ayca Coskunpinar, Jennifer L. Steiner, and Melissa A. Cyders, "Understanding Differences in Sexting Behaviors across Gender, Relationship Status, and Sexual Identity, and the Role of Expectancies in Sexting," *Cyberpsychology, Behavior, and Social Networking* 16, no. 8 (2013): 568–574.

28. I could not find statistics on the number or percent of suicides by women that are directly connected to the circulation of image-based abuse. What is clear is that Parsons's case is not unique. Since her suicide in 2013, there have been several other high-profile incidents in which image-based abuse appears to have been the primary factor leading to suicide. These include a widely publicized Italian case (BBC News, "Tiziana Cantone: Suicide following Years of Humiliation Online Stuns Italy," Sept. 16, 2016, http://www.bbc.com/news /world-europe-37380704). Underreporting combined with a hodgepodge of laws, which make the production of "consensual porn" legal in some jurisdictions

and not others, further confound attempts to identify the relation between suicide and image-based abuse.

29. According to the Centers for Disease Control and Prevention (CDC), 11 percent of all alcohol consumed in the United States is consumed by people between the ages of twelve and twenty, despite the fact that they are under legal drinking age, and more than 90 percent of this alcohol is consumed in the form of "binge drinks" (CDC, "Fact Sheet—Underage Drinking," Oct. 20, 2016, https://www.cdc.gov/alcohol/fact-sheets/underage-drinking.htm). In a 2017 study, the CDC found that 7 percent of U.S. women reported experiencing a completed rape as a minor. Sharon G. Smith, Jieru Chen, Kathleen C. Basile, et al., *The National Intimate Partner and Sexual Violence Survey, 2010–2012 State Report* (Atlanta: Centers for Disease Control and Prevention, 2017), 167, https://www.cdc.gov/violenceprevention/pdf/NISVS-StateReportBook.pdf.

30. Although the boys were eventually charged with the circulation of child pornography, they were never charged with assault. In his review of the case, Murray D. Segal, an independent investigator, concluded that "While ironic, it is likely true that had there not been more information to investigate [photographic evidence of the incident], the suspects would have been charged with sexual assault on the sole basis of Rehtaeh's statement(s)." Murray D. Segal, "Independent Review of the Police and Prosecution Response to the Rehtaeh Parsons," Oct. 8, 2015, p. 48, https://novascotia.ca/segalreport/Parsons -Independent-Review.pdf.

31. Ibid., 40.

32. Silvan Tomkins, *Shame and Its Sisters: A Silvan Tomkins Reader*, ed. Eve Kosofsky Sedgwick and Adam Frank (Durham, NC: Duke University Press, 1995), 134–136.

33. For example, in the Rehtaeh Parsons case, the victim transferred schools twice, but the photo at the center of her case continued to follow her into new social contexts (Segal, "Independent Review of the Police and Prosecution Response," 13).

34. David Cantor et al., *Report on the AAU Campus Climate Survey on Sexual Assault and Sexual Misconduct* (Rockville, MD: Association of American Universities, 2015), https://www.aau.edu/sites/default/files/AAU-Files/Key Issues/Campus-Safety/AAU-Campus-Climate-Survey-FINAL-10-20-17.pdf. The report also found that one-third of women had experienced nonconsensual sexual contact at least once by their senior year of college.

35. Shawn Michelle Smith and Sharon Sliwinski observe that there is a long history of theorists leaning on optical metaphors to explain the unconscious mind, but "Sigmund Freud was one of the first to intuit this idea. He began using photographic processes as a metaphor for his concept of the unconscious mind as early as 1900." Smith and Sliwinski, "Introduction," in *Photography and the Optical Unconscious,* ed. Shawn Michelle Smith and Sharon Sliwinski (Durham, NC: Duke University Press, 2017), 1.

36. David L. Smith, "The Mirror Image of the Present: Freud's Theory of Retrogressive Screen Memories," *Psychoanalytische Perspectieven* 39 (2000): 7.

37. Sigmund Freud, "Screen Memories" (1899), facsimile edition, reprinted in *On Freud's "Screen Memories,"* ed. Gail S. Reed and Howard B. Levine (London: Karnac, 2015), 24.

38. Ibid.

39. Phyllis Greenacre, *Trauma, Growth and Personality* (1952; repr., New York: International Universities Press, 1969), 191.

40. Gail S. Reed and Howard B. Levine, "Screen Memories: A Reintroduction," in *On Freud's "Screen Memories,"* ed. Reed and Levine, 29.

41. See in particular Lucy Lafarge, "The Screen Memory and the Act of Remembering," in *On Freud's "Screen Memories,"* ed. Reed and Levine, 36–57.

42. Freud, "Screen Memories," 7.

43. Donna J. Bridge and Joel L. Voss, "Hippocampal Binding of Novel Information with Dominant Memory Traces Can Support Both Memory Stability and Change," *Journal of Neuroscience* 34, no. 6 (2014): 2203–2213.

Chapter Four. When Tagged Subjects Leave Home

1. Nick Strayer, "The Great Out-of-State Migration: Where Students Go," *New York Times,* Aug. 26, 2016.

2. Joshua Meyrowitz, *No Sense of Place: The Impact of Electronic Media on Social Behavior* (New York: Oxford University Press, 1985), viii, 28, 5, 6.

3. Ibid., vii.

4. Jodi Kantor and Catrin Einhorn, "What Does It Mean to Help One Family?" *New York Times,* Sept. 8, 2016.

5. Chia-chen Yang and B. Bradford Brown, "Motives for Using Facebook, Patterns of Facebook Activities, and Late Adolescents' Social Adjustment to College," *Journal of Youth and Adolescence* 42, no. 3 (2013): 403–416.

6. Aristotle, *The History of Animals*, book 13: 16.

7. Peter Berthold, *Bird Migration: A General Survey*, 2nd ed. (Oxford: Oxford University Press, 2001), 12.

8. Mark R. Fuller and Todd K. Fuller, "Radio Telemetry Equipment and Applications for Carnivores," in *Carnivore Ecology and Conservation: A Handbook of Techniques*, ed. Luigi Boitani and Roger A. Powell (Oxford: Oxford University Press, 2012), 152.

9. Sam Howe Verhovek, "Ethical Issues Arise in Boom in Pet Microchips," *New York Times*, June 12, 1999.

10. Although tagging or inserting tracking devices into humans has never been widely accepted, there are a few exceptions. There is the long and troubling history of marking some humans (those who have been enslaved) with brands or tattoos. And in the 1970s, the U.S. criminal justice system started to use electronic tracking devices to monitor individuals on parole. This form of tagging has frequently been welcomed (even by many prison reformers) as a progressive alternative to extended prison sentences, rather than viewed as an infringement of privacy. Barton L. Ingraham and Gerald W. Smith, "The Use of Electronics in the Observation and Control of Human Behavior and Its Possible Use in Rehabilitation and Parole," *Issues in Criminology* 7, no. 2 (1972): 35–53.

11. Dan Collins, "Florida Family Takes Computer Chip Trip," CBS News, May 10, 2002, http://www.cbsnews.com/news/fla-family-takes-computer-chip-trip/.

12. Lev Grossman, "Meet the Chipsons," *Time*, Mar. 11, 2002, 56–57; Smith quoted in Julia Scheeres, "They Want Their Own ID Chips Now," *Wired*, Feb. 6, 2002, https://www.wired.com/2002/02/they-want-their-id-chips-now.

13. In early 2017, for example, a Swedish startup began to implant employees with microchips that opened doors and could be used to complete routine tasks, such as logging onto photocopiers. To encourage the practice, which was not required, the company held a "chipping party" for any employee who agreed to have a chip implanted. Associated Press, "Cyborgs at Work: Swedish Employees Getting Implanted with Microchips," *The Telegraph*, Apr. 4, 2017. While the company's practice gained considerable news attention, not all the

attention was positive. An article in the *New York Times* detailed the potential problems such implants might pose in the future, which range from excessive monitoring of employee behaviors (e.g., the length of their bathroom breaks) to the creation of new avenues for hacking. Maggie Astor, "Microchip Implants for Employees? One Company Says Yes," *New York Times,* July 27, 2017.

14. Hiawatha Bray, *You Are Here: From the Compass to GPS, the History and Future of How We Find Ourselves* (New York: Basic Books, 2014).

15. In a 2006 article in the *New York Times,* David Pogue wrote about the interest among parents in tracking their children: "Let's face it: we're in love with the idea of secret location trackers.... Many parents may have fleetingly harbored the fantasy of equipping their children with such tracking devices.... This is one sci-fi gadget that's no longer fi, thanks to advanced sci—satellite-based tracking based on Global Positioning System (G.P.S.) technology. At least five companies ... have built G.P.S. tracking into something children carry voluntarily: cellphones." Pogue, "Cellphones That Track Kids," *New York Times,* Dec. 21, 2006, C1.

16. Given the history of tagging, it is not entirely insignificant that some companies, such as Trax (developer of one of the most popular consumer tracking devices used by families with young children), market the same technologies to both parents and pet owners. See the Trax homepage for details: https://traxfamily.com.

17. Clay Shirky, *Here Comes Everyone: The Power of Organizing without Organizations* (New York: Penguin, 2008), 310.

18. The looming information overload problem was both a public and private crisis. While public archives and libraries were certainly grappling with the issue, so too were ordinary people as their own collections of photographs started to multiply at an increasingly rapid pace. See Dario Teixeira, Wim Verhaegh, and Miguel Ferreira, "An Integrated Framework for Supporting Photo Retrieval Activities in Home Environments," *Ambient Intelligence,* Proceedings of the First European Symposium, EUSAI 2003, ed. E. Aarts et al. (Berlin: Springer, 2003), 288–303, quotation on 288.

19. Ethan Todras-Whitehill, "'Folksonomy' Carries Classifieds beyond SWF and 'For Sale,'" *New York Times,* Oct. 5, 2005.

20. Quoted in Wade Roush, "Tagging Is It," *MIT Technology Review,* June 1, 2005, https://www.technologyreview.com/s/404210/tagging-is-it/.

21. Clay Shirky, "Ontology Is Overrated: Categories, Links, and Tags," n.d., Clay Shirky's Writings about the Internet, http://shirky.com/writings/ontology -overrated.html.

22. Facebook, "Making Phototagging Easier," June 30, 2011, https://www .facebook.com/notes/facebook/making-photo-tagging-easier/467145887130/.

23. Steven Heyman, "Photos, Photos Everywhere," *New York Times,* July 29, 2015.

24. Kevin J. O'Brien, "Germany Investigating Facebook Tagging Feature," *New York Times,* Aug. 4, 2011, B4.

25. Somini Sengupta and Kevin J. O'Brien, "Facebook Can ID Faces, but Using Them Grows Tricky," *New York Times,* Sept. 22, 2012, A1; Somini Sengupta, "Facebook Acquires Israeli Facial Recognition Company," *New York Times,* June 18, 2012.

26. Rose Eveleth, "How Many Photographs of You Are Out There in the World?" *Atlantic,* Nov. 2, 2015.

27. Robinson Mayer, "Anti-Surveillance Camouflage for Your Face," *Atlantic,* July 24, 2014. As facial recognition and automated tagging have developed, activist designers have started to develop methods to undermine these technologies, including innovative fabrics that effectively overwhelm or confuse the algorithms designed to search for faces in photographs. See the Berlin-based designer Adam Harvey's HyperFace Camouflage project, https://ahprojects.com /projects/hyperface.

28. Tim Moynihan reported in *Wired* in late 2016 that Google's PhotoScan app was designed to help users take better digital photographs of all the old analogue photographs they have accumulating in photo albums and shoeboxes. Moynihan explains, "Once it's captured, a photo is backed up online and added to your Google Photos library. . . . It'll be a great showcase for Google Photos' facial recognition over time; the app is already really good at identifying the same person over the course of their life with its computer vision, and the onslaught of old scanned photos should be a brand-new test for the app's impressive AI." Moynihan, "Google Just Made It Way Easier to Scan Your Own Photos," *Wired,* Nov. 15, 2016, https://www.wired.com/2016/11/google-photoscan-app-scan -your-old-photos.

29. To put the value of Facebook's photo assets into perspective, consider just one of its recent acquisitions. Instagram was developed in 2010 with about half a million dollars in startup funding. Within two years, Facebook bought the company, which still had no real revenue stream, for $1 billion in cash and stocks. Facebook wasn't just acquiring a competitor, but also Instagram's massive trove of tagged photographs—a purchase that would help to drive Facebook's research and development on facial recognition. See Victor Luckerson, "Here's Proof That Instagram Was One of the Smartest Acquisitions Ever," *Time*, Apr. 19, 2016, http://time.com/4299297/instagram-facebook-revenue.

30. In April 2017, Mark Zuckerberg told attendees at his annual developers' conference that Facebook was planning to build user-friendly augmented reality (AR) applications, beginning with applications that could be experienced through mobile phones. For example, people might be able to review a restaurant by posting virtual notes with suggestions about what to order. However, the convergence of social media and AR could lead to a world where not only texts and photographs but also places and things are taggable. These data-rich artifacts have the potential to profoundly change our visibility in the present, past, and future.

31. When copy machines were first introduced in the 1960s, for example, Xerox marketed the machines to male office managers and executives as a cost-efficient and accurate alternative to employing a receptionist—that is, effectively rendering women's paid office labor redundant. In the end, women were not replaced by copy machines, but office labor was profoundly restructured in ways that were, at least initially, highly gendered. See Kate Eichhorn, *Adjusted Margin: Art, Activism, and Xerography in the Late Twentieth Century* (Cambridge, MA: MIT Press, 2016).

Chapter Five. In Pursuit of Digital Disappearance

1. Danielle Collobert, *It Then*, trans. Norma Cole (Oakland, CA: O Books, 1989), 9.

2. The book, *Chants de Guerres*, was reissued by the French publisher Calligrammes in 1999.

3. In the United States, the Supreme Court has held that because of First Amendment rights, the truthful publication of the identity of a juvenile cannot be punished. See Smith v. Daily Mail Publishing Co., 443 U.S. 97, 103 (1979).

4. In the United Kingdom, for example, Baroness Beeban Kidron, a British filmmaker and activist, spearheaded a framework referred to as 5Rights, which calls for the establishment of five rules that aim to make the internet a safer and more empowering space for children and adolescents. The first rule is the "right to remove": "Every child and young person should have the right to easily edit or delete all content they have created." Unfortunately, the campaign has also been accompanied by frightening statistics and accounts about how widespread cyberbullying is and how at risk children are online. This, the campaign insists, is because despite young people's depiction as "digital natives," they are in fact "on the lower 'rungs' of digital understanding" and "lack the skills and knowledge necessary to benefit from the immense opportunities on offer, or to understand the potential outcomes of their digital interactions, as they move between spaces that are either heavily limited or 'locked down,' and others where 'anything goes.'" Baroness Beeban Kidron, 5Rights Report, https:// d1qmdf3vop2l07.cloudfront.net/eggplant-cherry.cloudvent.net/compressed/04 cd865a83931874b36510d15f05a08d.pdf.

5. EU General Data Protection Regulation (GDPR) Article 17, "Right to Erasure ('Right to Be Forgotten')," Intersoft Consulting AG, n.d., https://gdpr -info.eu/art-17-gdpr/.

6. Although children sometimes appear on reality television programs (often without the same protections as other child actors), their numbers are few. Child reality television stars' experiences do, however, mirror the experiences of young social media celebrities. In both cases, the conditions of the exposure appear to circumvent established labor laws and regulations designed to protect child entertainers. Adam P. Greenberg, "Reality's Kids: Are Children Who Participate on Reality Television Shows Covered under the Fair Labor Standards Act?" *Southern California Law Review* 82, no. 3 (2009): 595–648.

7. danah boyd, *It's Complicated: The Social Lives of Networked Teens* (New Haven: Yale University Press, 2014), 57.

8. Jessica Kulynych, "No Playing in the Public Sphere: Democratic Theory and the Exclusion of Children," *Social Theory and Practice* 27, no. 2 (2001): 231–264.

9. Sonia Livingstone, John Carr, and Jasmina Byrne, "One in Three: Internet Governance and Children's Rights," Innocenti Discussion Paper no. 2016-01, UNICEF Office of Research, Florence, 7, https://www.unicef-irc.org /publications/795-one-in-three-internet-governance-and-childrens-rights .html.

10. When Facebook purchased Instagram in 2012, the company had yet to report any profits and had only thirteen employees. What Facebook bought was a company that had already captured the photo-sharing market and was showing signs of continued growth. The purchase was essential for Facebook, since the company was already pursuing facial recognition as a key part of its business strategy. Josh Constine and Kim Mai Cutler, "Facebook Buys Instagram for $1 Billion, Turns Budding Rival into Its Standalone Photo App," TechCrunch, Apr. 9, 2012, https://techcrunch.com/2012/04/09/facebook-to -acquire-instagram-for-1-billion.

11. Jodi Dean, *Democracy and Other Neoliberal Fantasies: Communicative Capitalism and Left Politics* (Durham, NC: Duke University Press, 2009).

12. Jodi Dean, "Big Data: Accumulations and Enclosure," *Theory & Event* 19, no. 3 (2016), https://muse.jhu.edu/article/623988.

13. David Harvey, "The 'New' Imperialism: Accumulation by Dispossession," *Socialist Register* 40 (2004): 63–87.

14. Dean, "Big Data."

15. Simon Nørby, "Why Forget? On the Adaptive Value of Memory Loss," *Perspectives on Psychological Science* 10, no. 5 (2015): 562.

16. Dean, "Big Data."

17. Snapchat Support, "Snapstreaks," https://support.snapchat.com/en-US/a /Snaps-snapstreak.

18. Mary H. K. Choi, "Like. Flirt. Ghost.: A Journey into the Social Media Lives of Teens," *Wired,* August 25, 2016, https://www.wired.com/2016/08/how-teens -use-social-media.

19. Olivia Solon, "Facebook Says Cambridge Analytica May Have Gained 37m More Users' Data," *Guardian,* Apr. 4, 2018.

20. For a detailed account of the debt collection business, see Jake Halpern, "Paper Boys: Inside the Dark, Labyrinthine, and Extremely Lucrative World of Consumer Debt Collection," *New York Times Magazine,* Aug. 15, 2014.

21. Kaplan Test Prep found that 29 percent of college admissions officers had carried out an online search of an applicant, 31 percent had visited an applicant's Facebook page or another social networking page, and 30 percent had discovered something that negatively affected the applicant's admissions chances. Kaplan Test Prep, "Kaplan Test Prep Survey: More College Admissions Officers Checking Applicants' Digital Trails, But Most Students Unconcerned,"

news release, Oct. 31, 2013, http://press.kaptest.com/press-releases/kaplan-test
-prep-survey-more-college-admissions-officers-checking-applicants-digital
-trails-but-most-students-unconcerned. Cornerstone Reputation reported that
36 percent of admissions officers searched applicants online, 67 percent looked
up applicants on Facebook, and 40 percent found content that left a negative
impression. Cornerstone Reputation, "The 2016 Cornerstone Reputation
Admissions Survey," press release, https://www.prnewswire.com/news
-releases/cornerstone-survey-indicates-steadying-of-trend-in-college
-admissions-officers-reviewing-students-online-300231674.html. But
Cornerstone Reputation is evidently invested in promoting the idea that college
admissions officers are looking at potential applicants' digital footprints, since it
is in the business of providing digital reputation management services to college
applicants.

22. Hannah Natanson, "Harvard Rescinds Acceptances for At Least Ten
Students for Obscene Memes," *Harvard Crimson*, June 5, 2017, http://www
.thecrimson.com/article/2017/6/5/2021-offers-rescinded-memes/.

23. Katie Davis and Emily C. Weinstein, "Identity Development in a Digital Age:
An Eriksonian Perspective," in *Identity, Sexuality, and Relationships among
Emerging Adults in the Digital Age*, ed. Michelle F. Wright (Hershey, PA: IGI
Global, 2017), 13.

24. See Viktor Mayer-Schönberger's discussion of "digital abstinence" in
Delete: The Virtue of Forgetting in a Digital Age (Princeton: Princeton University Press, 2009), 128–132.

25. Henry Jenkins, "Empowering Children in the Digital Age: Towards a
Radical Media Pedagogy," *Radical Teacher* no. 50 (Spring 1997): 30–35.

26. AdSense is just one of the many avenues for placing advertisements on a
social media site. Profits are based on both page views and clicks, and site
owners share profits with Google. In order for someone under eighteen to open
an AdSense account and begin to make money directly from a social media site,
a parent or adult guardian must not only consent to the account opening but
also have a social media site and an AdSense account. That is, a minor cannot
monetize a social media site without consent from an adult. See Google
AdSense eligibility guidelines: https://support.google.com/adsense/answer
/9724?hl=en.

Conclusion

1. While some companies are using data to drive their own research and development on artificial intelligence and machine learning, other companies, such as Acxiom, CoreLogic, Datalogix, and ID Analytics, specialize in collecting, analyzing, and selling data about consumer activities to other companies.

2. Erik Erikson, *Childhood and Society*, 2nd ed. (New York: Norton, 1963), 262.

3. Nancy Jo Sales, *American Girls: Social Media and the Secret Lives of Teenagers* (New York: Vintage, 2016), 62.

ACKNOWLEDGMENTS

Most of this book was written at the New York Society Library. I thank the library's staff for making this historic institution such a productive space for writers and readers in the present. This book also benefited from the pro bono reference librarian support offered by my friend Jenna Freedman and from the research assistance of Andrea Nappi and Neve Diaz-Carr. At Harvard University Press, Andrew Kinney offered feedback on the manuscript at several key points, and I am especially grateful to him for sharing my enthusiasm for this project as it evolved. I also wish to thank Louise Robbins for her feedback and editorial intervention later in the process. My greatest debt is to my partner in life and ideas, Angela Carr, whom I thank for reading and offering editorial advice on this book and for her love, listening, and logic.

INDEX